T0266850

A little body are many parts

Un cuerpecito son muchas partes

Legna Rodríguez Iglesias

A little body are many parts

Un cuerpecito son muchas partes

Translated by Abigail Parry and Serafina Vick

BLOODAXE BOOKS

Poems © Legna Rodríguez Iglesias
Translations © Abigail Parry and Serafina Vick
Introduction © Serafina Vick

ISBN: 978-1-78037-496-3

First published in 2019 by
Bloodaxe Books Ltd
Eastburn
South Park
Hexham
Northumberland NE46 1BS

in association with
The Poetry Translation Centre Ltd
The Albany, Douglas Way
London SE8 4AG

www.bloodaxebooks.com
www.poetrytranslation.org

This book has been selected to receive financial assistance from English
PEN's PEN Translates programme, supported by Arts Council England. Eng-
lish PEN exists to promote literature and our understanding of it, to uphold
writers' freedoms around the world, to campaign against the persecution
and imprisonment of writers for stating their views, and to promote the
friendly co-operation of writers and the free exchange of ideas.
www.englishpen.org

Designed in Albertina by Tattersall Hammarling & Silk
Cover design by Tattersall Hammarling & Silk
Printed in the UK by Bell & Bain Ltd, Glasgow, Scotland on acid-free paper
sourced from mills with FSC chain of custody certification

Contents

INTRODUCTION

This Girl from Camagüey

Legna was born in Camagüey in central Cuba in 1984 and currently lives in Miami, Florida. As well as poetry she has written theatre, short stories, children's books and a novel. Her poetry has been translated into Portuguese, German, Italian and English, and *A little body are many parts* will be the most comprehensive anthology of her poetry in any language. This bilingual anthology features a selection of poems from all eight of Legna's collections, offering readers a thorough insight into the oeuvre of this prolific poet. Where cultural translation has proved impossible, we have included some explanatory notes, which you will find at the end of the collection.

Legna has always written; she was first published in her early twenties, bursting onto the Cuban literary scene with all the ferocity of a stampeding elephant. A contemporary Cuban artist told me: 'Suddenly, out of nowhere, this girl from Camagüey was winning all the literary prizes. Her poetry was unmistakably unique, so personal and shocking.' Legna's highly original voice attracted notice and over the next decade or so she was awarded a number of prestigious prizes, both at home and abroad. In 2015 Legna moved to Miami, where she continues to receive literary acclaim. Her first novel, *My Favourite Girlfriend was a French Bulldog*, is being published in the USA this year.

Contemporary Cuban poetry is as diverse and indefinable as contemporary poetry in any other country, but Legna does belong to a particular generation of poets. *Generación O*, formed mainly of poets born after 1975, is founded on the shared experience of growing up after the fall of the Soviet Union, when Cuba was launched into extreme deprivation. Up until the late 1980s, post-revolutionary Cuban poetry was tied to the regime, glorifying the new society being built with unfettered idealism. In the 1980s, Cuban poets began to turn away from the *coloquialismo* and *conversationalismo* – the adoption of colloquial, conversational language in poetry to better communicate with the proletariat – that had dominated the three decades following the revolution.

After this first rupture came the *Diáspora* movement of the early 1990s, a group of poets, many of them living outside Cuba, who sought radically to transform the face of Cuban poetry. With *Diáspora* as their predecessors, *Generación O* have no rules to break, indeed the only rule for them seems to be that there are no rules. Born long after the heady days of Castro's revolution, *Generación O* embody the disenchantment of their parents and grandparents. No style, form or ideology binds these poets together, and it's this lack of coherence that best reflects the chaos and loss of hope in a country where waiters earn more than surgeons.

Dancing the Macarena with Galileo

Though Legna refers to herself as 'the docile dog of Cuban poetry', her work is innately rebellious. She has never sought to please anybody, writing from a deeply personal perspective that's often hard to follow and/or stomach. Legna has no truck with poetic norms, often mocking them, as in the poem 'I wanted to do some sort of poetic exercise' from the collection *Gum*:

> so I decided to compose this poem
> while falling from a chimney
> a disastrous idea
> as the word poem and the word chimney

sound very similar
so you're not allowed to write them together

The speaker goes on to describe her 'blackened tongue', a ludic echo of the 'golden tongue' described by both Keats and Browning. Legna seems to be mirroring a distorted image of Apollo; instead of spinning lyrical verse with a golden tongue, she is composing a farcical poem with a blackened one.

Legna's rebellious streak is most prevalent in her representation of men. The *grandfather* referenced in various of her collections can be seen not only as the shadow of Cuba's paternalist regime and all the homophobia and conservatism that goes with it, but also as an amalgamation of all the great literary and scientific men credited with creating the world she inhabits. Berthold Brecht, Oscar Niemeyer, Galileo, René Descartes, Matsuo Bashō, Albrecht Dürer and Martin Heidegger are but a few mentioned in this anthology. These men brush shoulders with the speaker, creating a proximity to the poet that is often ridiculous: Niemeyer is a fellow Sagittarius, Dürer painted her, Heidegger is spotted hopping off a collective truck near Camagüey, Galileo wants the speaker to dance the Macarena with him, Brecht becomes the speaker's grandfather and Bash her doppelgänger.

The speaker's numerous and often surreal encounters with these men do not feel aggressive, but nor are they completely innocent. By creating these bizarre and unlikely scenarios, the speaker seems to be underscoring the fact that these men did not construct the modern world with women like her in mind. God himself, the ultimate paternalist figure, only has words of condescension for the speaker when she fails to win a competition he'd promised she would, 'just kidding, gorgeous/ keep writing, gorgeous' ('When I send off poems to a competition' from the collection *Gum*). These words reverberate throughout Legna's collections, taunting the poet as she attempts to create a feminine space in a form created by men. In return, Legna taunts the male figures that appear in her poems, putting them in ridiculous situations and sometimes even scolding them:

> no, I can't dance the macarena with you, Galileo
> I've told you a thousand times, Galileo
> the macarena is a dance for satyrs and other sex-
> mad creatures

The dissentient relationship between Legna's speaker and men is best laid out in her poem 'Spoilt' from the collection *Fertile Truce* (2012). In this poem the speaker sets out guidelines for behaviour in relation to her grandfather:

> Bad behaviour:
> saying to grandfather
> *screw the fatherland*
>
> Good behaviour:
> saying to grandfather
> *hooray for the fatherland!*
>
> All the while
> saying to grandfather
> *your country is my country*

The speaker sets up a simple dichotomy, either she can do what grandfather wants, or she can piss him off. There is no middle ground. Within this tension between pleasing and displeasing, the speaker is seeking recognition, reminding grandfather that they share a country, that they are, in fact, equal. The final lines read:

> Bad behaviour:
> to laugh.

> Good behaviour:
> to clean the blood from his nails.

Here the poetic voice reveals that if she chooses good behaviour she is complicit in her grandfather's violence, cleaning the blood from under his nails. Alternatively, she can laugh, presumably at her grandfather and his bloody nails. I read this poem as a promise of bad behaviour; the speaker knows that toeing the line means betraying herself, so laughing, rebelling, must be the only dignified way out.

Not a Tasty Dish

One of the elements present throughout all eight of Legna's collections is her fascination with symbology. This is most obvious in her 2012 collection, *The Perfect Moment*, where isolated objects and symbols abound. Indeed, the first poem featured from *The Perfect Moment* in this anthology, 'The Day that I', revolves around five objects: a river, a plank, a curl of excrement, a golden cup and the speaker's head. These five objects switch places continuously, one on top of the other, the other on top of one, until the last four lines:

> inside my head
> the chickens of disquiet, pecking
> happily
> endlessly

The poem leads us in a spiral motion down towards the speaker's own mind, where indeed, the endless whirlpool of objects began. Legna seems to be asking the reader: what more is a human mind, than an eternal swill of signifiers? This collection in particular basks in the tension between signifier and signified. In 'Red Room' the speaker is with a rhinoceros, a mare, a woman and a woodpecker:

and almost all of us
look like what we are
the rhinoceros looks like what she is
the mare looks like what she is
the woman looks like what she is
the woodpecker – I mean come on

as for me
I'm just a little fish in the sea
or perhaps a little flag in the air
or perhaps a viper in the desert
I look like a real elephant
living
beneath the sign of Cassiopeia.

The other creatures merely appear to be what they are, there is never any confirmation that they actually are what the speaker says the are, signifier and signified never find perfect unity. Despite this, the others are still considered more complete than the speaker herself as she flits between possible signifiers; is she a fish, a flag, an elephant? As with 'The Day that I', the speaker is asking the reader, what is a being, if not a transient collection of signifiers?

This play with signs and symbols recurs again and again in Legna's poems under various guises, the most prominent of which is her own innate system of signs born of her life experience. Cuba is a world onto itself, and the island's state of isolation was ingrained into the collective imagination when the Soviet Union collapsed, leaving Cuba seemingly friendless. Legna, born in 1984, lived her formative years during Cuba's *special period outside of war* (1989 until the early 2000s), when the island was struggling to survive. This was a devastating time for Cubans; food shortages and power cuts were the norm, and hunger was a familiar sensation. Abandoned by the Soviets, Castro's Cuba could now only look to itself for sustenance. This inward gaze spread to all parts of society, creating a nation that saw itself as alpha and omega. With this introversion arose a system of symbols peculiar not just to Cubans, as there were plenty living outside of the island, but specifically to those who lived through those harsh years. Legna's work is imbued with such symbols, for example, in 'Giddy-up Johnny' from the collection *Miami Century Fox*, the final tercet reads as follows:

> if we get to the edge of the chalk perimeter
> I'll wipe out its boundary forever.
> Adios, *queso proceso*. So long, pizza.

'Queso proceso' is a kind of processed cheese found only in Cuba, it's incredibly pungent and melts easily. It came to prominence during the Special Period, and was added to pizzas, pasta and whatever else it could squirm its way into. Nowadays you don't see it as much, but it lives on as a fond/painful memory of those times. The pizza the speaker is waving goodbye to is also a special kind of pizza, the kind 'an Italian wouldn't recognise'[1]: about two inches thick and covered in a greasy layer of a ketchup-type substance and 'queso proceso'. These pizzas

---

1   Pedro Juan Gutiérrez, *Dirty Havana Trilogy*, Ecco Press, 2002, p.37.

were a staple of the Special Period, where flavour wasn't the priority, being full was. These last lines then, can be taken as a farewell to Cuba, to hardship and bad pizza.

Another example of this Cuban code can be found in the poem 'Special Period' from the collection *Fertile Truce* (2012), where the poetic voice plays on the other meaning of the word *period*. The speaker begins the poem by describing a drop of menstrual blood creeping from her forehead downwards. This is uncomfortable to begin with, as the menstrual blood seems to be in the wrong part of the body, making the reader think more of blood from a head wound than blood flowing from the uterus. In typical Legna style, half way through the poem focus is severed completely from the menstrual drop and we're now presented with a window through which we see two kinds of fish, tilapias and tench. It's now the speaker's nose that becomes the poem's subject:

My nose points towards destiny
it hums the theme song
it holds silence
it transforms –

just like the tilapias
it transforms.

This half of the poem seemingly has no connection whatsoever with the first ten lines, the poem itself transforms, just like the tilapias. The first part at least references menstrual blood and ties in with the title, but now what's all this about fish? Tilapias, intensively farmed in Cuba, were a staple of the Special Period diet. Referenced in the Bible and highly revered in Ancient Egypt, tilapias don't have such a shining reputation in Cuba. As

Legna herself told me, 'the tilapia is synonymous with hunger in Cuba. It's not a tasty dish like it is in other places. It's the only thing on the menu.'

During the Special Period Cuban housewives were jokingly referred to as magicians, as they were able to go into the kitchen with seemingly nothing and reappear with a meal for an entire family. Dull tilapias were transformed into a nutritious treat at a time when animal protein was scarce. However, not even a survivor of the Special Period would necessarily see the connection between menstruation, fish and transformation. Legna does not write so that her audience says 'ahhh' in understanding, she writes so that your forehead wrinkles in perplexity and you're left wondering what all that was about. She wants you to come back and visit again soon. Legna recognises that the system of signs she has created is perhaps unintelligible, to fellow Cubans and to anyone else. I read the poem 'Blue Room' from *The Perfect Moment* as a kind of consolation to her readers:

> the language of the elephants
> is like a scream of terror
> this is why my madness
> sounds like sense to all pachyderms

There is method to her madness, and if you're willing to brush up on your pachyderm, you'll find Legna's work holds a treasure-trove of wisdom, wit and sharp-eyed insight.

Midnight Revelations and Bath-time Breakthroughs

'Abigail', my Whatsapp voice note started, 'I'm going to sound completely bonkers…' I had woken up convinced I had found the solution to one of our translation conundrums in my sleep, only to find what had seemed a stroke of genius was actually completely banal and altogether useless. Abigail had more luck in the bath, where her translation muse tended to visit her. Between these personal revelations, long Whatsapp chats between London and Havana and a constant to-ing and fro-ing of drafts, Abigail and I have arrived at an English rendition of Legna's work that we're truly proud of. The process has been everything I could have hoped for: educational, thought-provoking, and most importantly, entertaining.

Abigail and I come from very different perspectives, and I found it thrilling to see her poet's eyes and ears at work. As both poet and translator, Abigail is fascinated by words, and would meticulously search for an adequate equivalent to carry over not just the meaning of a word, but its connotations and unique sound. Abigail would magically find a way to give her translations their own life, transposing the original but creating something altogether different. The result is English translations that read like original poems, with their own rhythms, riddles and word plays.

As a Cuban resident, my role was to place Legna's work in context for Abigail. I was there to reveal hidden secrets, like the aural insinuation of 'bollo' (Cuban slang for vagina) in the line 'la cabeza comiéndoselo vivo' (NO SE DICE/ from *Miami Century Fox*) or the huge cultural implications of the term 'afuera', detailed in our translation notes. Abigail would then take this knowledge and use it to find a solution. If she couldn't then we'd have another discussion and knock our heads together until something fell out.

Legna, Abigail and I all share a healthy sense of humour, and it was sometimes through clowning about that Abigail and I came to the right solution for our translation. In the poem 'Orange Room' from the collection 'The Perfect Moment', there is a pumpkin chorus that likes to remind us of its existence. It was only through reading the poem out together and jokingly chanting 'luminous pumpkins do, oh yes' that we came to add these extra two syllables to the first line of the chorus. In Spanish the line that's twice repeated by the pumpkin chorus reads 'las calabazas lumínicas sí'; we felt this repeated affirmation, 'sí', gave us license to embellish the chorus with a playful 'oh yes' reminiscent of many a childhood sing-a-long.

Another time humour prevailed was in our translation of 'When a 25-day-old cat dies' from the collection *Gum*. The original poem is written in the impersonal third person; the subject of the poem is 'uno', or 'one'. Legna uses the impersonal third person to create ambiguity between the subject, who is supposedly preparing itself for the cat's death, and the 'someone' who threw it out of the window twelve hours earlier. The repetition of the verb 'tirar' (to throw) makes us think it may well have been the very same 'uno' that threw the cat out the window who is now preparing to threw it in the bin. The third person impersonal is used far more to speak generally in Spanish that it is in English, whereas the use of 'one' in English sounds distinctly old-fashioned. In reaction to my initial literal translation which used the general you in English, Abigail offered two versions of the poem, one using a mixture of 'you' and 'one' and another using 'one' throughout. I was instantly convinced by the latter version, whose tone reminiscent of an early twentieth-century pamphlet, 'one is prepared', perfectly captured the playfulness of the original.

Serafina Vick

Tregua Fecunda
Fertile Truce

Tregua Fecunda

Sobre el ataúd de mi *grandfather*
hay flores nacionales
ese hombre luchó en una guerra
hace más de sesenta años
una guerra por la libertad
liberarse de lo que lo ata
es la lucha común.
Sabía leer y escribir
con cierta facilidad
pero no mejor que yo
fue una lástima
que quien practica la autopsia
le dejara el marcapasos
en el fondo de su pecho
ahora bajo las flores
hay un marcapasos vigilándome
¿Qué esperaba mi *grandfather* de mí?
¿Qué sembrara una flor nacional
en el fondo de mi corazón mangrino?
Que en paz descanses *grandfather*
ya escribí cosas *grandfather*
y esa es la mejor revolución
que haré.

Fertile Truce

There are national flowers
on my *grandfather*'s coffin.
This man fought in a war
more than sixty years ago.
A war for freedom.
Freeing yourself from that which binds you
is the common struggle.
He knew how to read and write
and had some aptitude for it.
But not like me.
It's a pity
that whoever performed the autopsy
left his pacemaker
buried deep in his chest
and now, beneath those flowers,
there's a pacemaker keeping time with me.
What did my *grandfather* expect?
That the seed of a national flower
would plant itself deep in my churlish heart?
Rest in peace, *grandfather*.
I've been writing, *grandfather*.
And that is *my* revolution.

La memoria es un tren bala

Si pongo una copa de agua a la altura de mi frente
sobre una superficie más o menos plana
alguien que murió por mí en algún lugar de la memoria
despertará y me guiará hacia afuera.
De acuerdo a la cantidad de los que hayan muerto por mí
será la cantidad de copas a la altura de mi frente
sobre una superficie más o menos plana.
Mientras más copas más llanto
afuera es tierra flores llanto
Alejandro Iglesias
tierra
María Novoa
flores
Ángel Iglesias Novoa
llanto
Julián Moronta
tierra
Esperanza Pacheco
flores
Luisa Roselia Moronta Pacheco
llanto.
Seis copas
seis semillas de marañón mexicano
si pongo una semilla a la altura de mi frente nadie despertará
nadie me guiará hacia afuera
adentro o afuera es la misma cosa.

Memory is a bullet train

If I place a glass of water at head height
on a more or less flat surface
someone who died for me somewhere in memory
will wake up and take me away.
The number of glasses placed at head height
on a more or less flat surface
will equal the tally of those who have died for me.
More glasses, more weeping.
Away is *earth, flowers, weeping.*

Alejandro Iglesias
earth
María Novoa
flowers
Ángel Iglesias Novoa
weeping
Julián Moronta
earth
Esperanza Pacheco
flowers
Luisa Roselia Moronta Pacheco
weeping

Six glasses.
Six Mexican cashew nuts.
If I place a nut at head height, no one wakes up.
No one takes me away.
Here and *away* are exactly the same.

Treinta cabezas diarias

Ella quería
venir a mi patria
a jugar con los símbolos
y los animales patrios
a meterse en mi mar
como un avestruz
en otro avestruz
hijo y padre
atorándose.
Ella quería bailar el mambo
bailar el mambo
definitivamente.
Yo quería
ir a su patria
a jugar con cualquier cosa
dame unas tijeras
y verás
cómo acabo
con todo.

Thirty heads a day

She wanted
to come to my country
to play with its symbols
and with all the national animals
and to get in the sea
like an ostrich
burying its head
in another ostrich
father and son
throttling each other.
She wanted to dance mambo
to dance mambo
definitively.
I wanted
to go to her country
and play with any old thing.
Hand me those scissors
and watch me
let rip.

Mala crianza

Lo mal hecho
decirle a *grandfather*
abajo la patria.
Lo bien hecho
decirle a *grandfather*
arriba la patria.
Entretanto
decirle a *grandfather*
tu patria es mi patria.
Al otro día por la mañana
churre
vacío
pan viejo
sangre
Camagüey
Tínima
sangre
Hatibonico
churre
sangre en las uñas churrosas de *grandfather*.
Lo mal hecho
reír.
Lo bien hecho
quitarle la sangre a las uñas.

Spoilt

Bad behaviour:
saying to grandfather
screw the fatherland

Good behaviour:
saying to grandfather
hooray for the fatherland

All the while
saying to grandfather
your country is my country

The morning after:
grime
emptiness
stale bread
blood
Camagüey
Tínima
blood
Hatibonico
blood under grandfather's grubby nails.

Bad behaviour:
to laugh.

Good behaviour:
to clean the blood from his nails.

Período especial

La gota de menstruación que resbala por mi sien
se parece a las gotas incansables de lluvia
o a las lágrimas del tocororo
la gota de menstruación rueda por mi nariz
moja mis labios
y vuelve
igual que yo me coloco
en el centro de una idea
esta es la idea:
menstruar para siempre
por la mirilla veo tilapias
tencas
mi nariz atisba el sino
tararea la canción
contiene al silencio
transfigura
igual que las tilapias
transfigura.

Special Period

The drop of menstrual blood that travels down my temple
is like one of the endless drops of rain
or the tears of the *tocororo*.
The drop of menstrual blood rolls down my nose
wets my lips
and returns to me
just as I situate myself
in the centre of an idea.
Here's the idea:
to menstruate forever.
Through the peephole I spy tilapias,
tench.
My nose points towards destiny
it hums the theme song
it holds silence
it transforms –

just like the tilapias
it transforms.

Come

Suave y deliciosa
la palabra tenca viaja
de la mano de quien la vende
a la mano de quien la compra
yo soy quien la compra
y aquí tenemos
como en el amor
un triángulo
un sistema
un juego
una educación
una historia
un pasado
un presente
un futuro
un beneficio
y aquí tenemos
como en el amor
una tregua
fecunda.

Eat

Smooth and delicious
the word *tench* travels
from the hand of whoever sells it
to the hand of whoever buys it.
I'm the one buying it
and here we have
– as in love –
a triangle
a system
a game
an education
a story
a past
a present
a future
a boon
and here we have
– as in love –
a fertile truce.

Cereza podrida

Uno cree que al bajar
La Avenida de Los Presidentes
va a sentir alivio
seguridad
tal vez admiración
o por el contrario náusea
pero uno no siente ni pinga
el océano a lo lejos es lo más pesado que hay
un cielo en la tierra
un valle de agua por gusto
atraviezo la Avenida
sintiendo todo lo que puedo sentir
y un niño me grita loca porque hablo sola
me hablaba a mí misma del amor
de los deseos que tengo de que chupen mi cereza
pero yo no estoy para menores
yo podría despingar a su madre con mi puño
y luego echarla al océano
con todos los presidentes
mirándome.

Rotten cherry

You'd think you'd feel at ease
walking down the Avenue of Presidents
you'd think you'd feel safe
perhaps impressed
perhaps nauseated
but actually you feel fuck all.
The ocean at one end is the weightiest thing here
an earthbound sky
a valley of water for no good reason.

I cross the Avenue
feeling everything I can feel
and a kid shouts that I'm crazy because I'm talking to myself.
I was telling myself about love –
of how much I want my cherry sucked.
But I'm not for minors
and I could fuck his mum up with my fist
and throw her in the ocean
with all the Presidents
just staring at me.

Jauría loca

¡Cómo me gustan los signos de exclamación!
¡Cómo me gusta exclamar!
¡Cómo me alegra vivir entre perros!
¡Sarnosos!
¡Húmedos perros de la virtud que por la noche lamen la luna!
¡Tétricos perros del frenesí que por el día también lamen la luna!
¡La luna hay que lamerla siempre!
¡Chuparla si es preciso!
¡Cómo me gusta comprarle perros al que más caro los venda!
¡Cómo me gusta el sol!
¡Cómo me gusta la tierra!
¡Cómo me gusta la nieve!
¡Que nunca he visto la nieve!
¿Es la nieve pesada o liviana?
¡Cómo me pica el pellejo!
¡Y me sacudo!
¡Y me sacudo!

Mad dog pack

How I love exclamation marks!
How I love to exclaim!
How happy I am to live among dogs!
Mangy dogs!
Dank dogs of virtue that lick the moon by night!
Dismal dogs of frenzy that lick the moon by day!
The moon must always be licked!
Suck it if you have to!
How I love to buy dogs at the highest price possible!
How I love the sun!
How I love the earth!
How I love snow!
I've never seen snow!
Is snow heavy or light?
How my skin itches!
And I shake!
And I shake!

El cementerio

Todos formaban un grupo de hombres y mujeres revolucionarios
nacieron a partir de la segunda década del siglo veinte
para ser revolucionarios en un país revolucionario
y amar a su país más que a sus hijos
y amar a su país más que a sus madres
y verlo despojado de cadenas
murieron a partir de los primeros años del siglo veintiuno
con la agonía revolucionaria de los hombres y mujeres
que han contemplado orgullosos el amor
fueron enterrados en tumbas de cemento
que cuando llueve se filtran.

The cemetery

They were a group of revolutionary men and women
born in or after the second decade of the twentieth century
to be revolutionaries in a revolutionary country
and love their country more than their children
and love their country more than their mothers
and see it stripped of its chains.
They died in or after the first years of the twenty-first century
with the revolutionary agony of men and women
who have proudly countenanced love;
they were buried in concrete tombs
and when it rains
they leak.

Canaán

Sobre los hombros del Año de La Reforma Agraria:
una palma irreal.
Sobre los hombros del Año de La Planificación:
un ángulo.
Sobre los hombros del Año del Esfuerzo Decisivo:
una letrina.
Sobre los hombros del Año de Los Diez Millones:
un televisor.
Sobre los hombros del Año del VeinLcinco Aniversario del Triunfo:
un nacimiento.
Sobre los hombros del Año del Centenario de La Caída:
todos los héroes de la historia
un hombre triste encabeza la lista
la tristeza es lo peor.
Sobre los hombros del Año de Los Héroes:
una idea.
Sobre los hombros del Año de La Revolución Energética:
un viaje.
Sobre los hombros del Año Cincuenta de La Revolución:
una corriente.
Sobre los hombros del Año en Curso:
una mano escribiendo cualquier cosa.
Quien escribe cualquier cosa
es capaz de todo.

Canaan

On the shoulders of the Year of Agrarian Reform,
an unroyal palm
On the shoulders of the Year of Planning,
an angle
On the shoulders of the Year of Decisive Force,
a latrine
On the shoulders of the Year of Ten Million,
a television set
On the shoulders of the Year of the Twenty-fifth Anniversary of the
    Triumph of the Revolution,
a birth
On the shoulders of the Year of the Centenary of the Death of José Martí,
all the heroes of history
with a sad man at the top of the pile.
Sadness is the worst.
On the shoulders of the Year of Heroes,
an idea.
On the shoulders of the Year of the Energy Revolution,
a journey.
On the shoulders of the Year of the Fiftieth Anniversary of the Revolution,
a current.
On the shoulders of the current year,
a hand, writing.

The hand that writes
is capable of anything.

Transtucé
Transtucted

47

Perdóname Esmeralda
perdóname Vertientes
perdóname Guáimaro
perdóname Nuevitas
perdóname Piedrecitas
perdóname Sierra de Cubitas
perdóname Céspedes
perdóname Sibanicú
perdóname Jimaguayú
perdóname Minas
perdóname Najasa
perdóname Florida

todavía
no he mirado
los altos edificios
ni la nieve
ni el fango

y no los miraré
hasta que ustedes
me den
la venia.

47

Forgive me Esmeralda
forgive me Vertientes
forgive me Guáimaro
forgive me Nuevitas
forgive me Piedrecitas
forgive me Sierra de Cubitas
forgive me Céspedes
forgive me Sibanicú
forgive me Minas
forgive me Najasa
forgive me Florida

I still
have not looked upon
those tall buildings
nor the snow
nor the mud

and I will not
look upon them
until you
give me permission.

52

Ni a la nieve
ni al cine
he logrado
asistir

ni a tu casa
ni al cine
he logrado
asistir

ni a tu casa
ni al bosque de tu casa
ni al oso de tu casa
que vuelve a ti
en primavera

ni a ti
en primavera
he logrado
acercarme

como al mar
que lo miro
de lejos
y veo
otra cosa.

52

I have not managed
to see to the snow
or go to the cinema

I have not managed
to see to your house
or go to the cinema

not your house
not the forest of your house
not the bear of your house
which returns to you
in springtime

I have not managed
to come to you
in springtime

like the sea
which I look at
from afar, seeing something
that is not the sea.

53

Meter un dedo en el agua
es una oración
de sexto grado

formada por
un sujeto y
un predicado

aparentemente simple

tan simple que nunca
llego a saber
si ese dedo
es mi dedo

a qué se refiere
cuando dice agua

a qué se refiere
cuando dice meter

qué sucede
en la oración

qué otras cosas
sucederían.

53

Dipping a finger
                    in the water
is a sentence
from sixth grade

made up of
a subject
and a predicate

seemingly simple

so simple, in fact,
that I never get to find out
if the finger in question
is my finger

what the *water*
refers to

what the *dip*
refers to

what is going on
in the sentence

what else
            would happen.

54

Yo vi a Heidegger
comprando una botella
de agua
en Esmeralda

lo vi
comprando huevos
en Guáimaro

lo vi
comprando frutas
en Vertientes

lo vi
leyendo un libro
en el ferrocarril
de Nuevitas

lo vi
azuzando a un perro
en Piedrecitas

lo vi
en Sierra de Cubitas
con una sierra
en la izquierda
no sabía
que el tipo
fuera ambidiestro

lo seguí viendo
en Céspedes
esta vez
me pareció que no

54

I saw Heidegger
buying a bottle of water
in Esmeralda

I saw him
buying eggs
in Guáimaro

I saw him
buying fruit
in Vertientes

I saw him
reading a book
on a train from Nuevitas

I saw him
goading a dog
in Piedrecitas

I saw him
in Sierra de Cubitas
with a saw
in his left hand
I never knew
the guy was ambidextrous

I saw him again
in Céspedes
only this time
it seemed to me
he wasn't feeling well

I saw him again

se sentía bien

lo seguí viendo
en Sibanicú
haciendo lo mismo
que en Jimaguayú
como si tal cosa
fuera involuntaria

lo seguí viendo
en Minas
al bajarme
de un camión
Heidegger también
se bajó del camion

lo vi
abriendo una sombrilla
en Najasa

llovía
y había sol
en Florida

más allá.

in Sibanicú
doing the same thing
he was doing in Jimaguayú
as if the thing he was doing
was involuntary

I saw him again
in Minas
as I was getting off
the back of a truck

Heidegger, too,
was getting off
the back of the truck

I saw him
opening an umbrella
in Najasa

it was raining
and it was sunny
in Florida

further beyond.

55

Lavadoras de Manhattan
no me dejan
meter
por la ranura
la misma tarjeta
que meto en Miami

secadoras de Manhattan
no me dejan
meter
por la ranura
la misma tarjeta
que meto en Miami

tengo mi ranura
bien cerrada

los territorios
son discriminatorios.

55

Washing machines in Manhattan
do not let me put
the same ticket
in the slot
that I put in the slots in Miami

Tumble dryers in Manhattan
do not let me put
the same ticket
in the slot
that I put in the slots in Miami

I keep my slot
tight shut.

Territories
tend to discriminate.

57

Están por todos lados
nos van a comer
nos van a exterminar

ni siquera la falta
de pan sirio
en la mesa
me preocupa

ni siquiera el presidente
su feúra
me preocupa

ni siquiera la ropa
de los niños
que no han nacido
me preocupa

frente a ellos
metiendo las narices
en mi casa
y en mi cama
y en la cuna de los niños
que no han nacido
casi nada
me preocupa

tengo que buscar
en Google
cómo deshacerme
de ellos.

57

They are all around us
they are going to eat us
they are going to exterminate us

not even the lack
of flatbread
on the table
worries me now

not even the president
and his ugliness
worries me now

not even the clothes
for the children
who have yet to be born
worry me now

not compared to them
poking their noses
into my house
into my bed
into the cradles of children
who have yet to be born
almost nothing
worries me now

I must have a look
on Google
to find out
how to get rid of them.

66

La idea era
interpretar
la libertad sexual
como un fenómeno
psicosocial

déjame preguntarlo
antes de que mañana
yo haya cambiado
y sea otra

por qué la mayoría
de los filósofos
más importantes
son alemanes

por qué la mentalidad moderna
se basa en obedecer
las órdenes
que se nos dan

por qué
no has vuelto
a escribirme

un tigre
ripió mis botas
estoy descalza
en la nieve.

66

The idea was
to interpret
sexual freedom
as a psychosocial
phenomenon.

Let me ask you now
because tomorrow
I will have changed
into someone else

why is it
that the majority
of the most important philosophers
are German

why is it
that our modern way of thinking
is based on obeying
the rules
we're given

why
have you not
written back to me

a tiger
has shredded
my boots

I am barefoot
in the snow.

Miami Century Fox
Miami Century Fox

Estábamos chateando en Facebook
y tú me preguntas cuántos poemas pienso incluir en este libro,
y yo te digo que tal vez cincuentiuno, para no extenderme mucho,
porque los poemas con rima siempre me han parecido monótonos,
o tal vez cincuenta y nueve, porque es el año en que triunfó una Revolución,
y tú me dices ¡Patria o muerte (unidos), venceremos!

Pueblo gusano

¡Que pase por aquí el pueblo gusano!,
aullaba una mujer en el pasillo.
Sostenía en la mano su martillo
y en la otra una hoz. El aeroplane

desde el que aterrizara muy temprano
con mochila y laptop y lazarillo
se detuvo de golpe como un grillo
sobre tecla/península de piano.

Vi el teatro más feo. Vi la guerra.
Una escena más cómica que trágica.
Una niña, una yegua y una perra

iban casi llorando. Tarde mágica.
Un ratón disparó contra la perra.
Me dio risa y melindre. Tarde mágica.

We were chatting on Facebook
and you asked me how many poems I was planning on putting in this book
and I said maybe fifty-one, so as not to overexert myself,
because rhyming poems always sound a bit monotonous to me,
or maybe fifty-nine, because that's the year a Revolution triumphed,
and you said *Homeland or death, (united) we shall overcome!*

Maggot people

This way, maggot people!
bawled the woman in the corridor.
In one hand she held her hammer,
in the other she held a sickle.

Early this morning I came in on a plane
with a laptop, a guide and a rucksack.
It came to a stop like a cricket
on the key (the *peninsula*) of a piano.

I saw the ugliest theatre. I saw war.
A spectacle less tragic than comedic.
I saw a girl, a dog and a horse

on the brink of tears. Magic kingdom.
A mouse shot the dog. That tickled me, sure,
made me squirm. Magic kingdom.

¿Un alien posee un ancestro?
¿Quién es el abuelo del alien?
En caso de ser un no-alien,
¿existe también un no-ancestro?

Ms Trolley recuerda países

Entonces, para no hacer largo el cuento
me dijeron su caso está aprobado
aunque es caso pendiente, delicado.
Y salí más tranquila, pero lento.

Desde cama/sofá, con desaliento,
recordé las ciudades donde he estado,
Mozambique, París, Tokio, Belgrado.
Solo en mapa y en sueños, no te miento.

Mi caso era un mal caso porque yo
tuviera la mirada que tuviera
tal vez decía sí cuando era no.

Y miraba a los ojos a cualquiera
porque fue lo que daddy me enseñó
seas alien o seas extranjera.

Does an alien have an ancestor?
Who is an alien's grandfather?
In the case of a non-alien,
is there a non-ancestor?

Ms Trolley remembers countries

Well, in a nutshell: *they tell me*
they've approved your application
<u>*provisionally*</u>*. There were complications.*
And I left feeling calmer. Slowly.

[Settled / dejected] on [a sofa / a bed]
I thought of the cities I've visited.
Mozambique, Tokyo, Paris, Belgrade –
I've been there [on maps / in my head].

Mine was a difficult case, you see,
because I have that look. You know the one –
it seems to say *yes*, but really

means *no*. And I look everyone
dead in the eye, like my *daddy* taught me,
whether foreigner, stranger, or alien.

Fue la primera vez,
en un período de treinta años,
que sentarse en una silla estomatológica
requeriría trescientos dólares.
Eso, y la impresión de que el hombre
lo había hecho todo mal.

El día que a mi novia le empezaron a doler las muelas

Tenía tanto pánico al doctor
como verse rodeada de serpientes
en zoológico negro, de serpientes
que te pasan la lengua alrededor.

Tenía tanto pánico, y peor
por tratarse de sus únicos dientes.
Algo insólito en días decadentes
donde el miedo no es forma ni color.

Le sudaba la nuca. Se asustaba
con la aguja fatal de la anestesia.
Se moría un momento. Me llamaba.

Yo acudía. La tonta estaba recia.
Más recia de lo que me imaginaba.
Golpeé duro. Después, nube y amnesia.

For the first time in thirty years,
sitting in a dentist's chair
would cost three hundred dollars.
That, and the feeling
that the guy was doing it all wrong.

The day my girlfriend's molars started hurting

She was so afraid of the doctor –
as if she were circled by snakes
in a black zoo with circling snakes
flickering their tongues all over her.

She was so afraid. And what's more,
the teeth were all hers. Just imagine.
An extraordinary thing, in a decadent age
where fear has no form and no colour.

Sweat on the back of her neck. And dread –
dread for that fatal needle of anaesthesia.
She called out to me then, half-dead

and I came to her side. She's a ninny,
but she was tougher than I'd imagined.
I struck hard. Then clouds and amnesia.

Que te agarren por el cuello y te lo digan.
Por primera vez.
Y veas, por primera vez,
que te equivocaste.

No se dice

Me vengo (fue su voz) puta, cojones.
Pero no me sonaba repulsivo.
Palabras son palabras. Sustantivo
se pone como es. ¡Cómo te pones!

Me vengo (cuarta vez) puta, cojones.
Su cabeza comiéndoselo vivo.
Palabras son memorias. Sustantivo
no sabe traicionar aunque traiciones.

Memoria sobre mí, bajo de mí,
a mi lado, conmigo en una esquina.
Palabra que me gusta y aprendí.

Espérate, cojones. Vaselina.
Su cabeza comiendo carmesí
es palabra, semiótica, y espina.

When they grab you by the throat and say it.
For the very first time.
And you see, for the very first time
that you've made a mistake.

You don't say

I'm coming (said the voice) *ohfuckohfuckohfuck I'm –*
But it didn't sound wrong.
A word is a word. A noun
you must take as it comes. As *you* come!

I'm coming (fourth time) *ohfuckohfuckohfuck I'm –*
The head, eating it alive. A word is a memory.
A noun does not know how to betray,
but it may betray all the same.

Memory on top of me, memory under.
Memory alongside, in a corner with me.
A word that I liked, a word I'll remember.

Wait – *bollocks.* Vaseline.
The head eating roseate crimson
is linguistic, semiotic, and thorny.

¿Qué pasa con la música?
¿Qué tiene?
¿Qué significa para un ser humano,
abatido, cansado, sobrio,
experimentar el dolor
de la música en la cabeza?

Jazz neto

Hay jazz en Coral Gables, gratis jazz,
así que voy corriendo, eso es lo mío.
Son tres viejitos gordos, Murphy Trío,
y en el público, tres mil viejos más.

Es mediodía y miércoles. Atrás
Salzedo y Aragón forman un lío
de autos y semáforos. Un crío
me ve desde la hierba. Cuánta paz.

Al fin el calvo de la batería
se pone a improvisar junto al del bajo.
Es gratis, por favor, y es mediodía.

Si disfrutas, no coges peste a grajo.
Alégrate, lubrica la alegría,
o sal a conseguir algún trabajo.

What is it about music?
What's it got?
What does it mean
for a depressed, tired, sober human being
to feel the pain of music in their head?

Pure Jazz

There's jazz in Coral Gables at noon –
it's free, and it's my thing, so I run.
The Murphy Trio: three fat old men
playing for an audience of fat old men.

Noon on a Wednesday. Behind us,
Salzedo and Aragon is gridlocked.
Stop signs. Engines. Horns. A child
watches from the grass. Such peace.

Then the bald guy on drums gets cracking,
jamming with the guy on bass. Hey,
it's free, and it's noon for fuckssake,

and sweat doesn't stink when you're happy.
So get stuck in, joyful and slick,
or piss off and do something else with your day.

Los juguetes que flotan en el agua,
si son de goma o plásticos,
y tienen alguna grieta o rajadura
pueden llegar a convertirse
en una figura parecida a mí.
Aunque yo no floto en el agua.
Ni soy de goma o plástica.

La cabeza que se llenó de agua

Hubo un día que a mí me la cortaron
y rodó por la grava la pelota,
que no era pelota y sí una mota
de algodón y saliva. La cortaron

porque se molestó. La demacraron.
Le quitaron el pico a la gaviota.
Ese día dormí como marmota
sin mi pico y sin ti. Me desguazaron.

Me llené. Me inundé. Me quedé viva.
Fue expandiéndose sobre los manteles
la mitad de una taza de saliva.

Sobre los azafranes, los laureles,
sobre flores guerreras, desde arriba,
desde abajo, sin ti, sin decibeles.

Those toys that float on water –
if they're rubber or plastic,
and have some sort of split or crack,
they can end up looking
a bit like me.
Though I don't float on water.
And I'm not rubber or plastic.

The head that filled with water

And then one day they cut it off.
It rolled over the gravel – a ball
that wasn't a ball but a tangle
of cotton and spit. They cut it off

when it got upset. They wrecked it.
They broke the beak off the seagull.
And that day, I slept like a dead girl
with no beak, and no you. I was in bits.

I filled up. Overflowed. Stayed alive.
And spreading out over the table,
the linen – a saucerful of saliva.

Over the saffron, over the laurels,
over the flowers of war. From above,
from below, without you, without decibels.

Uno es su nombre.
Demasiada gente ya ha hablado sobre eso
y sobre la connotación de eso
y sobre la noción del ser
que implica el nombre,
lo nombrado.
Sin embargo, cuando el mismo nombre
es pronunciado de otra forma
ha ocurrido un fenómeno
que no es ni fuga ni transformación.
Es una perturbación.

What is my name?

Al decir tengo hambre, tengo hambre.
Al decir tengo miedo, tengo miedo.
Al decir tengo hambre y tengo miedo
las dos piernas me tiemblan de calambre.

¿Si me tapo la boca tendré hambre?
¿Si me coso los labios tendré miedo?
Desenróscase lengua cuando cedo
como rollo de púas y de alambre.

Y al decir tengo hija y tengo hijo
no se oye la voz, no pasa nada.
No me pongo contenta ni me aflijo.

Y al decir tengo rabia y tengo espada
pareciera que digo un acertijo,
pero cuándo, si siempre estoy callada.

We are our names.
Lots of people have already discussed this
and the connotations of it
and the notion of the being
implied by the name:
the named thing.
However, when the same name
is pronounced another way
a phenomenon occurs
which is neither a transformation nor an escape.
It's a disturbance.

What is my name?

When I say that I'm hungry, I'm hungry.
When I say that I'm scared, I'm scared.
When I say that I'm hungry and scared,
I tremble. My legs go beneath me.

If I stopper my mouth, am I hungry?
If I sew up my lips, am I scared?
Unravel, tongue, when I yield,
like a roll of barbed wire. Like a story.

When I speak of my daughter, my son,
nothing happens. My voice is not heard.
I feel nothing: not peace, not vexation.

When I say that I'm angry, that I have a sword,
perhaps it's a riddle I've spun.
But how – when I've not said a word?

A los slices se les puede poner más de seis ingredientes.
Y están los slices All the Way
que incluyen todos los ingredientes
menos el pollo, la piña, y las anchoas.
Poner anchoas en los slices
es asqueroso y desagradable.
Pero comerlas no.
A la gente le gusta hacer pedidos
que incluyan muchísimos ingredientes.
Mientras más sabores, mejor.
Como la luz.

Arre Johnny

Necesito reunir bastante *money*
para quedarme echada en mi rincón
cuatro días, cien días, un millón,
y salir a pasear sobre mi *pony*.

Arre Johnny, camina, arre Johnny.
Vayámonos bien lejos, corazón.
Aquí las cosas huelen a jamón,
a tocino y salchicha y pepperoni.

Hace tanto calor, tanto bochorno.
Arre papi, camina, tengo prisa.
Me quemé las dos manos en el horno.

Si llegamos al círculo de tiza
borraré para siempre su contorno.
Adiós queso proceso, goodbye pizza.

You can put more than six ingredients on *slices*.
Those are All the Way *slices*
and include every ingredient
except chicken, pineapple and anchovies.
Putting anchovies on the *slices* is horrible.
Eating them isn't, though.
People like to order things
that have loads of ingredients.
The more flavours, the better.
Just like light.

Giddy-up Johnny

I need to get together some *money*
so I can stay here in the corner
four days, a hundred, a million or more,
and go for a ride on my *pony*.

Giddy-up Johnny, let's go, Giddy-up Johnny,
let's go far away from here, darling.
Here everything smells of salami
and sliced ham and bacon and pepperoni.

It's so hot, so sticky. Not one minute longer.
I've burned both my hands on the toaster.
Go daddy-o, let's get out of here –

if we get to the edge of the chalk perimeter
I'll wipe out its boundary forever.
Adios, *queso proceso*. So long, pizza.

73

Este libro es un experimento.
Doloroso y cruel.
En todos los sentidos.
Por más que sumo y multiplico,
el muermo sale de mí,
y me rodea.

No me flores

Si me muero en Miami no me flores.
Si me muero en Miami carretera.
¿No recuerdas gentil azucarera
aquel tiempo? Los últimos amores

ya no vuelven jamás. Días mejores
que florecen debajo de la acera
por donde yo camino. Que se muera
el músculo, de penas y dolores.

Si me muero en Miami dame spray.
Si se muere mi oreja cómo sigo.
Si se muere en lo oscuro mi mamey.

Aquel tiempo dichoso fue contigo
miel de abeja, pan suave, Camagüey.
No me flores, gentil, sobre el ombligo.

This book is an experiment.
A painful and cruel one.
In every sense.
However much I add or take away
depression seeps out of me, surrounds me.

No flowers for me

No flowers, if I die in Miami.
If I die on the highways of Miami.
Don't you remember that sweet time,
my sugar? The love that's behind me

is gone. There are better days
under the pavement – they flourish
as I walk along. There's a muscle
for suffering and pain, that ought to die.

If I die in Miami, give me *spray*.
If my spark dies, how would I go on.
And if it dies in the dark – my *mammee*.

That sweet time – it was with you. Golden
honey, soft bread, and Camaguey.
No flowers, please, on my belly button.

75

El momento perfecto
The perfect moment

El día que me

Un río
una tabla sobre el río
un círculo de excremento sobre la tabla
una copa de oro sobre el círculo de excremento
mi cabeza sobre la copa de oro.
una tabla
un círculo de excremento sobre la tabla
una copa de oro sobre el círculo de excremento
mi cabeza sobre la copa de oro
un río sobre mi cabeza.
un círculo de excremento
una copa de oro sobre el círculo de excremento
mi cabeza sobre la copa de oro
un río sobre mi cabeza
una tabla sobre el río.
una copa de oro
mi cabeza sobre la copa de oro
un río sobre mi cabeza
una tabla sobre el río
un círculo de excremento sobre la tabla.
mi cabeza
un río sobre mi cabeza
una tabla sobre el río
un círculo de excremento sobre la tabla
una copa de oro sobre el círculo de excremento.
adentro de mi cabeza
las gallinas de la intranquilidad picando
alegremente
eternamente

The day that I

A river
a plank on the river
a curl of excrement on the plank
a golden cup on the curl of excrement
my head on the golden cup
a plank
a curl of excrement on the plank
a golden cup on the curl of excrement
my head on the golden cup
a river on my head
a curl of excrement
a golden cup on the curl of excrement
my head on the golden cup
a river on my head
a plank on the river
a golden cup
my head on the golden cup
a river on my head
a plank on the river
a curl of excrement on the plank
my head
a river on my head
a plank on the river
a curl of excrement on the plank
a golden cup on the curl of excrement
inside my head
the chickens of disquiet, pecking
happily
endlessly

La cabeza que perdí

Principalmente tu casa me inquieta/ la ciudad
    también me inquieta
pero es tu casa con sus diez habitaciones el motivo
    principal de mi inquietud
y en este punto acotaré que el fenómeno de la inquietud
es para mí un hábito/ pero no
    por ser un hábito llego a acostumbrarme/ a otros
hábitos sí me he acostumbrado:

leer varios capítulos De las Pasiones en General
    y de la Naturaleza del Hombre,
tomar un poco de leche hasta que la leche se me
    derrama por la barbilla,
vestirme de azul quemado o de amarillo quemado,
introducirme a la gran oficina,
quedarme atrapada entre los 4 vidrios calovares
hasta que los 4 vidrios calovares me vomitan hacia fuera,
cruzar la ciudad,
ir a tu casa

y en este punto acotaré que mientras cruzo la ciudad
el fenómeno de la inquietud comienza a manifestarse
con una exclusividad que solo yo experimento
lo sé por las encuestas, por la fachada de los hoteles
por los hombres que me saludan cómplices y mal
    peinados
soy lo que los hombres quieran ver y ellos son lo que
yo quiera ver

y en este punto acotaré que no por eso gusto de los hombres
ni los hombres gustan de mí/ puesto que formamos
parte de un histórico disgusto universal/ mientras
toco el timbre de la puerta de tu casa me imagino a tu
casa por dentro/ me imagino a ti por dentro y saco la

The head I lost

Mainly your house troubles me/ the city
   also troubles me
but your house with its ten rooms is the main
   cause of my disquiet

at this stage I should point out that the phenomenon of disquiet
is a habit of mine/ although
   the fact that it's a habit does not mean
   that I am accustomed to it/ there are other
habits to which I have become accustomed:

reading a few chapters of *Of the Passions in General,*
   and Incidentally of the Whole Nature of Man
drinking a little milk until the milk
   spills down my chin
dressing in burnt blue or burnt yellow
going into the big office
getting caught between the 4 sheets
   of one-way glass, until the 4 sheets of one-way glass spit me out
    again
crossing the city
going to your house

at this stage I should point out that it is when crossing the city
that the phenomenon of disquiet begins to manifest itself
exclusively and experienced only by me
I know it by investigation, by the entrances of hotels,
by the men who greet me, complicit
   and badly groomed
I am what men want to see and they are
what I want to see

at this stage I should point out that this doesn't mean men like me
nor that I like them/ given that we are part

mano del timbre

en cada una de las habitaciones se escucha una música
distinta: 1. Música clásica 2. Música africana 3. Música
árabe 4. Música japonesa 5. Música celta 6. Música hindú
7. Música española 8. Música de día 9. Música de
noche 10. Música para sacar agua de un pozo
y en este punto acotaré que sacar agua de un pozo
podría resultar definitivo
elijo donde se escucha la música japonesa

y en este punto acotaré que solo la mitad de uno
    de mis pabellones escucha
porque las otras ¾ partes que fueron creadas
    para escuchar
han perdido la audición desde el comienzo
cuando abriste la puerta con una mano
y con la otra quitaste de mi barbilla restos de leche
    del desayuno,
mientras oigo la música japonesa
capto lo que está sucediendo en este momento
    en este lugar
y soy el viejo Basho vestido de mujer joven
me voy convirtiendo en mí

y en este punto acotaré que todo el tiempo he sido yo
pero yo de cabeza
yo demasiado leve

of a historic and universal disgust/ while
pressing the doorbell of your house I imagine
the inside of your house/ I imagine you inside and I

take my finger off the doorbell
a different kind of music can be heard playing
in each of the rooms: 1. Classical music 2. African music
3. Arabic music 4. Japanese music 5. Celtic music 6. Hindu music
7. Spanish music 8. Day music 9. Night music
10. Music for drawing water from a well

at this stage I should point out that drawing water form a well
could well be decisive
I choose the room where Japanese music is playing

at this stage I should point out that only one half
    of one of my ears is listening
because the other ¾ which were
    made for listening
lost the ability to hear from the very beginning
from the moment you opened the door with one hand
and with the other wiped the last
    of the breakfast milk from my chin
as I listen to the Japanese music
I grasp what is happening in this very moment
    in this very place
and I'm old Bashō dressed as a young woman
I am turning into myself

at this stage I should point out that I've been me all along
but me headfirst
me, far too light

Música para camaleones

Si como, me duermo
y si me duermo, no escribo
si escribo acerca de la naturaleza, los animales vienen a mí
y si escribo acerca de la sociedad, otros animales
vienen a mí
prefiero los primeros animales
prefiero comer y dormir.
si voy en busca de experiencias nuevas, escribo
y si escribo, trasciendo
siempre adopto formas de la trascendencia
que jamás hubiera imaginado
un libro
una canción
una película experimental
buscar experiencias nuevas continúa pareciéndome
excitante.
si aúllo, me cazan
y si me cazan, desaparezco
tarde o temprano aullaré
tarde o temprano me cazarán
mi desaparición interferirá en todos los procesos
de la naturaleza
mi desaparición será arrolladora.
si mi desaparición será arrolladora, escribo
y si escribo, aúllo

Music for chameleons

When I eat, I fall sleep
and when I'm asleep, I don't write
when I write about nature, animals come to me
and when I write about society, other animals
come to me
I prefer the first kind of animal
I prefer eating and sleeping

when I go in search of new experiences, I write
and when I write, I expose myself
I always expose myself in ways
I never would have imagined
a book
a song
an experimental film
I still find the search for new experiences
exciting

when I howl, they hunt me
when they hunt me, I disappear
sooner or later I will howl
sooner or later they will hunt me
my disappearance will disrupt all natural processes
my disappearance will be dazzling
when I disappear dazzlingly, I write
and when I write, I howl

Red room

Estábamos las cinco:
la rinoceronta
la yegua
la mujer
la pájara carpintera
y yo
que soy la más preparada del grupo
juntas hicimos aquello
que nos pareció más agradable
lo hicimos en la mente
porque en la mente es donde sucede
lo que parece más agradable
y casi todas nosotras
parecemos lo que somos:
la rinoceronta parece lo que es
la yegua parece lo que es
la mujer parece lo que es
la pájara carpintera, por favor
pero yo
que solo soy una pecesita en el mar
o tal vez una banderita en el aire
o tal vez una víbora en el desierto
parezco una verdadera elefanta
viva
bajo el círculo
de Casiopea

Red room

There were five of us:
the rhinoceros
the mare
the woman
the woodpecker
and me
me, I'm the smartest of the group

together we did whatever
seemed nicest to do
we did it in our minds
because our minds were where
the things that seemed nicest happened

and almost all of us
look like what we are
the rhinoceros looks like what she is
the mare looks like what she is
the woman looks like what she is
the woodpecker – I mean come on

as for me
I'm just a little fish in the sea
or perhaps a little flag in the air
or perhaps a viper in the desert
I look like a real elephant
living
beneath the sign of Cassiopeia

Orange room

Antes bailaba con mi pareja de baile
en un sótano de velas y calabazas lumínicas
antes era antes
digería sobre todo frutas
sobre todo escondida bajo la cama
y los muelles de la cama me hacían sangrar el cráneo
y venían unas aves a tomarse aquellos líquidos
mi pareja de baile no existe
las calabazas lumínicas sí.
coro de calabazas:
las calabazas lumínicas sí
las calabazas lumínicas sí.
noto que se me han fracturado las muñecas
por volar detrás del pájaro de cartón
las fracturas están penadas por la ley
aquí muchas cosas están penadas por la ley
menos volar detrás del pájaro de cartón
lo que sucede es que el pájaro
jamás dejará que lo alcancen
el pájaro de cartón no existe
las calabazas lumínicas sí.
coro de calabazas:
las calabazas lumínicas sí
las calabazas lumínicas sí.
al cabo de media hora
empiezo a hacer bicicletas con los pies
el pie derecho hace las bicicletas a las mil maravillas
mientras que el pie izquierdo se demora notablemente
esto sin dudas me saca de quicio
el ojo derecho ve que amanece
mientras que el ojo izquierdo ve que anochece
ninguno de mis ojos existe
y ninguno de mis pies existe
las calabazas lumínicas sí.

Orange room

Before, I danced with my dance partner
in a cellar filled with candles and luminous pumpkins
before was before
I fed myself mostly on fruit
I mostly hid under the bed
and the bedsprings made my skull bleed
and some birds came and drank the liquid
my dance partner doesn't exist
but the luminous pumpkins do
Pumpkin chorus:

the luminous pumpkins do
oh yes
the luminous pumpkins do

I notice my wrists have fractured
from flapping after the cardboard bird
the fractures are punishable by law
here many things are punishable by law
though not flapping behind the cardboard bird
the thing is the bird
will never let you catch up with it
the cardboard bird doesn't exist
but the luminous pumpkins do.
Pumpkin chorus:

the luminous pumpkins do
oh yes
the luminous pumpkins do

After half an hour,
I start to peddle with my feet
my right foot peddles like a charm
while my left foot lags noticeably behind

coro de calabazas:
las calabazas lumínicas sí
las calabazas lumínicas sí

this obviously drives me mad
my right eye sees the day break
while my left eye sees the sun set
neither of my eyes exists
and neither of my feet exists
but the luminous pumpkins do.
Pumpkin chorus:

the luminous pumpkins do
oh yes
the luminous pumpkins do

Blue room

Los elefantes me hablaron
de un modo que no he logrado entender
yo estuve allí sentada casi en shock
casi calva ante los elefantes
cuando pienso en ellos
pierdo el control de las máquinas
como un grito de pavor
es el idioma de los elefantes
por eso mi locura se parece
al idioma de todos los paquidermos
en vano temo que los elefantes
desaparezcan para siempre de mi vida
mi vida es un lugar muy alumbrado:
platos
peinetas
personas
y pasiones
hay un elefante debajo de mi cama
intuí que el elefante había estado viviendo allí
incluso antes del raciocinio
mucho antes del estremecimiento

Blue room

The elephants spoke to me
in a way I have yet to comprehend
   I was sat there almost in shock
almost bald in front of the elephants

whenever I think of them
I lose control of the controls

the language of the elephants
is like a scream of terror
this is why my madness
sounds like sense to all pachyderms

pointlessly, I fear the elephants
will disappear altogether from my life
my life is a very well-lit place:
plates
pins
people
and passions

there is an elephant living under my bed
I sensed that the elephant was living there
faster than the speed of thought
and long before the shudder

White room

Magnificencia del pájaro inmóvil
que no quiere verme con ojos de pájaro
inmovilidad del ojo
recuerdo que morí en un armario de cedro
afuera del armario con una falda enorme
iba a callarme cuando abrí el armario
y quise meterme allí para encontrar las tres alas
del pájaro siniestro que no quiere verme
sino escamotearme
armario se llama el friso
donde estoy inmóvil como mis tres ojos

White Room

Splendour of the motionless bird
that doesn't want to see me with bird eyes

the eye, motionless

I remember I died in a cedar wardrobe
      outside the wardrobe with an enormous skirt
I was going to keep quiet when I opened the wardrobe
I wanted to go in to find the three wings
of the ill-omened bird that didn't want to see me
                but wanted to make me vanish

the frieze is called *wardrobe*
where I'm motionless like my three eyes

Chicle (ahora es cuando)
Gum (now is when)

'Cálmate…'

Cálmate
me digo
concéntrate
me digo
toma las riendas de tu vida
azuza a los perros
ordénales que corran
bien lejos de aquí
corre
me digo
bien lejos de aquí
me digo
sigue las señales de los perros
más allá del final
pero tú no querrás escribir
un solo poema en tu vida
tú querrás escribir mil poemas
por lo menos
escupe el chicle
me digo
tira el chicle
me digo
o masticas o tomas las riendas
es tu negocio.

'Calm down…'

Calm down
I tell myself
focus
I tell myself
take charge of your life
take up the reins
mush the dogs
and make them run
far, far away
run
I tell myself
far, far away
I tell myself
follow the dog tracks
where they stop, keep going
you won't want to write
one poem in this life
you'll want to write thousands
thousands at least

spit out that gum
I tell myself
bin the gum
I tell myself
you can chew
or take up the reins
it's up to you.

'Quería hacer un ejercicio poético…'

Quería hacer un ejercicio poético
que realmente me provocara sudar
así que decidí escribir este poema
cayendo desde una chimenea
algo desastroso
pues la palabra poema y la palabra chimenea
son parecidas en la sonoridad
y está prohibido escribirlas juntas
así que decidí escribir otro poema
cayendo desde otra chimenea
más lejana
para que las palabras también estuvieran distantes
pero no resultó
así que decidí escribir este poema
a pesar de todo
como lo había pensado desde el principio
cayendo desde una chimenea en tu mente
al final del poema
terminé con un brazo herido
con una lengua tiznada
con una risa feliz
por mi aptitud.

'I wanted to do some sort of poetic exercise…'

I wanted to do some sort of poetic exercise
that would really make me sweat
so I decided to compose this poem
while falling from a chimney
a disastrous idea
as the word *poem* and the word *chimney*
sound very similar
so you're not allowed to write them together
I therefore decided to write a different poem
while falling from a different chimney
one that was much further away
so that the words would also be further apart
but it didn't work
I therefore decided to write this poem
in spite of everything
and as I had meant to all along
falling from a chimney in your mind
at the end of the poem
I had a broken arm
and a blackened tongue
and a happy laugh
for my virtuosity.

'La que se estaba anudando…'

La que se estaba anudando
una soga en el pescuezo
le dijo a la que se iba a tirar
del quinto piso de su edificio:
a mí no me mires.

'Cuando un gato de 25 días fallece…'

Cuando un gato de 25 días fallece
uno está preparado para eso
mucho más si hace solo doce horas
alguien lo tiró por la ventana
como si fuera un poema estrujado
mal escrito
incluso si uno ve que el gato se acomoda
sobre el polvo del escritorio
sobre la agenda
y uno le dice al gato
no te cagues en la agenda
y hasta le pone un nombre
y hasta lo nutre con leche
sigue estando preparado para eso
uno está preparado para todo
envolver al gato con periódicos
tirarlo a la basura
quedarse pensativo
uno siempre se queda pensativo
después de que pasa algo
para lo que uno está preparado
a continuación uno se pregunta
si no ha sido mejor así.

'The one tying…'

The one tying
a noose around her neck
said to the one about to jump
from the fifth floor of the building:
don't look at me.

'When a 25-day-old cat dies…'

When a 25-day-old cat dies
one is prepared for it
even more so if only half a day ago
someone chucked it out of a window
as if it were a scrunched-up
badly written poem
and even if one has seen the cat making itself at home
on the dusty desk
on the diary
and has said to the cat
don't shit on the diary
and even if one has given it a name
and given it milk
one is still prepared for it
one is always prepared
wrapping the cat in newspaper
throwing it in the bin
lingering for a moment, pensive
one always lingers for a moment, pensive
whenever something has happened
for which one was prepared
and after that one says to oneself
it was for the best.

'*En el centro de cada ser hay un músculo traicionero…*'

En el centro de cada ser hay un músculo traicionero
un músculo que late, late, y nos guía
cuando ya no late, no nos guía
la muchacha de la que me apasioné
tenía sendas matas de pelo debajo de cada brazo
y el muchacho del que me apasioné
tenía pectorales más notables que mi pecho
después ellos dos se apasionaron juntos
en contra del raciocinio
afloró el triángulo
afloró la traición
afloró mi venganza cuando viéndolos tan amantes
los empastillé
y rasuré con una cuchilla sus sendas matas de pelo
y ponché con una aguja sus graciosos pectorales.

'At the core of every being…'

At the core of every being there is a treacherous muscle
a muscle that pulses, pulses, and guides us
when it stops pulsing, it no longer guides us
the girl I was madly in love with
had a generous tuft of hair under each arm
the boy I was madly in love with
had bigger tits than I did
next thing these two were madly in love with each other
and against all reason
the triangle flourished
betrayal flourished
my vengeance flourished, to see them so much in love
so I slipped them some pills
and I shaved off her generous tufts with a knife
and I popped his hilarious tits with a needle.

'Es una verdadera lástima…'

Es una verdadera lástima
que todos los artistas anteriores
hayan hablado del tiempo
con tanta virtud
en sus obras
todos
incluso los peores
han sentido cómo el tiempo
les revienta sus collares
los hace más tristes o más felices
y han hablado del tema
dominándolo
expandiéndose
por horas
yo solo gastaría algunas breves milésimas
para apoyar el lápiz
y escribir un punto.

'Cuando mando mis poemas a un concurso…'

Cuando mando mis poemas a un concurso
imagino a Dios diciéndome:
no te preocupes, belleza
ese dinero es tuyo
y duermo en paz
absoluta
más tarde
cuando el dinero pasa de largo
frente a mis ojos incrédulos
Dios me dice:
era una broma, belleza
sigue escribiendo, belleza.

'Truly, it is a shame…'

Truly, it is a shame
that all artists that came before us
have spoken of time
so powerfully
in their work
all of them
even the worst ones
have noticed time
breaking their necklaces
making them happy or unhappy
and they have discussed the topic
dominating it
dilating upon it
for hours
it would only take me a few brief thousandths of a second
to pick up a pencil
and write a full stop.

'When I send off my poems…'

When I send off my poems to a competition
I imagine God saying to me:
don't worry, gorgeous
that money's yours
and I sleep easy
in perfect
peace
later on
when the money walks by
right in front of my incredulous eyes
God says to me:
just kidding, gorgeous
keep writing, gorgeous.

'Te pido…'

Te pido
que no interpretes
los ámbitos culturales
porque sabrías
que soy la perra dócil de la poesía cubana
la perra sin hueso
ni sopa
hay otros perros
sarnosos
pero menos resquebrajados
menos dolidos
que yo
hay otros gatos también
te pido
que en paz me dejes
que tranquila me dejes
y sola
voy
a desenterrar
el hueso.

'I must ask you…'

I must ask you
not to mix
in cultural circles
because if you did
you would find out
I'm the docile dog of Cuban poetry
a dog without a bone
with no supper
there are other dogs
mangy ones
but less broken
less hurt
than me
there are also other cats
I ask you
to leave me in peace
to let me be

and alone
I will dig up
that bone.

Dame spray
Gimme spray

Kenozero

A nadie le importaría verme
sentada en la fila doce
del cine más importante de la ciudad
viendo una película rusa en una noche blanca
sobre un tipo que es cartero
con actores que no son actores
sino personajes de la vida cotidiana
de un lugar en el culo del perro

a orillas del lago tal.

A mitad de la película
el tipo comienza a ver un gato sobre su pecho.

A nadie le importaría que hubiera un gato en el cine
sentado en una butaca al lado de mi butaca
expresando emociones positivas con su cola.

A mitad de la película el gato de la película comienza a
mirarme de reojo.

A nadie le importaría llevarme a lo más hondo,
entre pinzas de mandíbula, sumergirme, enseñarme eso.

A ti qué te importaría.

Voy al cine de vez en cuando
y eso es demasiado importante para mí.

Kenozero

No one would even notice me
sitting in aisle twelve
of the most notable cinema in the city
on a white night, watching a Russian film
about a guy who's a postman
with actors who are not actors
but ordinary, everyday people
from the arse-end of nowhere

on the shores of lake something-or-other.

Halfway through the film, this guy
starts seeing a cat, sitting on his chest.

No one would care if there were a cat in the cinema
sitting in the seat next to mine
waving its tail felicitously.

Halfway through the film, the cat in the film
starts looking at me
out of the corner of its eye.

No one would think twice about taking me down,
between pincer-teeth, to the place
where the water is deepest.
To submerge me there. To teach me.

Does that mean anything to you.

I go to the cinema every now and then.
And that is everything to me.

El Gran Arquitecto

Con esta frase no me refiero a Dios
ni a mí, en particular, que publiqué aquel volumen
en el año dos mil trece
con el asombroso título de La gran arquitecta.
Mi homenaje en el poema es para Oscar Niemeyer
sagitario como yo del mismo día quince
del mismo mes diciembre
la misma cara de *yonofuí*.

Para él estas palabras,
escritas como si nada sobre un hormigón armado
que fue su obra y su pensamiento:
Es importante que sepas que estoy bajo los efectos de frutas
    desconocidas.
Hace tres días llegué a este país y quien me trajo me dijo come.
También el internet se ha convertido en fruta.
Lo que te den, cómetelo.
Me veo a mí misma en una pantalla mirando una puesta que vi hace
    diez horas.
Se acabó el tiempo. O mejor dicho, empezó.

Por eso estoy escondida tecleando en mi habitación.
Me escondo del internet y de todas esas frutas.
En la boca solo me cabe una fruta
pero ten la seguridad de que lo intentaré con dos.
Lo que escribo no es fruto de la creatividad.
Es fruto de la debilidad.
En la unión está la debilidad
y en la separación está la fuerza.

The Great Architect

By which I don't mean God,
nor me, in particular,
though I did publish that book in 2013
with the astonishing title *The Great Architect*.
No, the tribute in this poem goes to Oscar Niemeyer
a Sagittarius like me, born
on the same day (the 15th)
of the same month (December)
with the same *itwasntme* face.

These words are for him:
a mere trifle written on a block of reinforced concrete
which was his work and his philosophy.
You should know I am under the effect of unknown fruit.
I arrived in this country three days ago and the person who brought
    me here told me to eat.
The internet, too, has become a fruit.
You should eat whatever you can get.
I watch myself on a screen, watching
the same sunset I saw ten hours ago.
Time has run out. Or rather, it has begun.

That's why I'm hiding away in my room, typing.
I'm hiding from the internet and all that fruit.
I can only fit one fruit at a time in my mouth
but rest assured I will try to fit two.
What I write is not the fruit of creativity
it is the fruit of weakness.
In unity there is weakness
and in division, strength.

Un proceso acumulativo de materia seca que después de la floración es lento y se va intensificando durante la fase lechosa

El primer reloj de mi vida fue de juguete.
Las agujas se movían si yo movía la mano.

Los primeros zapatos de mi vida fueron ortopédicos.
Las agujas se movían si yo movía la mano.

El primer viaje de mi vida fue ilegal
La Habana-Lima y Lima-Santo Domingo
con una visa falsa bajo una tormenta llamada Ernesto.

El primer perfume de mi vida fue a los veintisiete años.
Jengibre francés, me parece.

Tengo un abuelo por parte de padre, llamado Ernesto.
Me parece.

An accumulation of dry matter that is slow after flowering but intensifies during the lactic phase

The first watch I ever had was a toy.
The hands moved whenever I moved my hand.

The first shoes I ever had were orthopaedic.
The hands moved whenever I moved my hand.

The first trip I ever took was illegal.
Havana-Lima and Lima-Santo Domingo
with a fake visa, in a storm called Ernesto.

The first perfume I ever had was at twenty-seven.
French Ginger, if I recall.

I have a grandfather on my father's side called Ernesto.
If I recall.

Mi novia se va hoy para Cancún

Mi novia se va hoy para Cancún.
Tiene miedo de que no nos veamos más.
No nos veremos más, estoy segura.
A los tres días de haber llegado un policía corrupto la llevará a la
    frontera.
Por el camino verá flores y lagartos del desierto.
Será una experiencia espectacular.
Las manos del policía se llevarán
a su casa ochocientos dólares.
Mi novia empezó a comerse una guayaba y un diente se le cayó.
Específicamente la muela que está al lado del colmillo.
Da la impresión de que tiene una piedra ahí.
Está nerviosa por el diente y yo estoy nerviosa
por la frontera.
Los dientes y las fronteras ponen los nervios de punta.

My girlfriend leaves for Cancún today

My girlfriend leaves for Cancún today.
She's scared we won't see each other again.
We won't see each other again, I'm certain.
Within three days of getting there
a crooked cop will take her to the border.
Along the way she will see desert flowers and lizards.
It will be a spectacular experience
                        and the pocket of the cop
will go home with eight hundred dollars in it.
My girlfriend started eating a guava and a tooth fell out.
Specifically, it was the molar that sits next to the canine.
Now she looks like she has a stone where the tooth was.
My girlfriend is worried about the tooth and I am worried
about the border.

Teeth and borders put us on edge.

El hermano de mi novia

El hermano de mi novia no parece una persona.
La forma de su cuerpo no es la de un ser humano.
Y eso me hace preguntarme
si la forma de mi cuerpo es la de un ser humano.
O por el contrario me parezco a mi cuñado,
un hombre sin pensamiento que necesita
irse de su país para poder sentir bienestar.
Está enamorado de una mujer como él sin pensamiento
que necesita irse de su país para poder sentir bienestar.
Y eso me hace preguntarme si alguna vez
he sentido bienestar dentro de mi país o fuera
o si necesito irme de él para poder sentirlo.
Es a lo que me refiero cuando digo
que el tipo no parece una persona
porque evidentemente tiene todo en su vida:
una mujer que lo ama.
Y eso me hace preguntarme si yo tengo todo en la vida.

My girlfriend's brother

My girlfriend's brother does not appear to be a real person.
The shape of his body is not that of a human being.
This makes me wonder
if the shape of my body is that of a human being
or if, in fact, I look like my brother-in-law,
a man so unimaginative he must leave his country
in order to feel well.
He's in love with a woman who is equally unimaginative,
who must leave her country
in order to feel well.
And this makes me wonder
if I have ever felt well, either in my country or out of it,
or if, in fact, I must leave my country in order to feel it.
This is what I mean when I say
that the guy does not appear to be a real person
because clearly he has everything in life:
                    a woman who loves him.
And that makes me wonder
if I, in fact, have everything in life.

Bachiller

Ayer se habló en titulares sobre la arquitectura vernácula,
forma de vivienda que abriga
techos de cinc y paredes de madera.
Me quedé pensando en ello toda la noche y parte de hoy
mañana fresca y propicia para el descanso, la teoría.
Es martes y aunque ovulando
me siento sobria, insensible,
un estado de relacionamiento
entre mi yo exterior y mi yo interior
que pudiera acoplarse a la ciencia, o por qué no,
a la arquitectura.
Nacida y criada en diseño indígena,
sentí vergüenza del hecho de no saber al respecto
sino la angustia que ofrecen,
fuera de lugar,
dos planchas bajo la lluvia.
Lluvia arrolladora,
convertida en vendavales,
ciclones, huracanes,
descrita por hombres, mujeres y niños,
con la siguiente expresión:
llovió más adentro que afuera.
Catástrofe, vacío, va sucediendo
en las casas aledañas a mi casa.
Los mayores te preguntan qué quieres ser al graduarte,
y tú dices sin dudarlo: carpintero.

Graduate

Yesterday the headlines mentioned *vernacular architecture*,
a kind of home involving
zinc roofs and wooden walls.
I thought about that all night and part of today.
The morning was fresh and (in theory)
a good morning for rest.
It's Tuesday – although ovulating,
I feel sober. Numb.
A state of equilibrium
between my interior and exterior selves
which might be down to science, or even (why not?)
to architecture.
Born and raised in the indigenous design,
I was ashamed to know nothing about it;
only the anguish
of two irons left out in the rain.
Overwhelming rain,
rain turned to gales,
cyclones and hurricanes, rain
described by men,
women and children as

raining more inside than out.

Disaster and ruin go on happening
in all the houses adjacent to mine.
They ask what you want to be when you're older
and you say, without blinking, *a carpenter.*

La cantidad inicial de agua que es necesario aportar al sustrato depende de la naturaleza de este y de sus dimensiones

Queridos escritores de todas partes del mundo,
tan maquillados y bien vestidos,
planchados y almidonados,
tímidos y excéntricos, no se demoren leyendo,
no lean más, deténganse. Tengan lástima del público,
altamente peligroso, que los escucha.
Tienen dientes de tiburón, de cocodrilo, de pantera,
de perro y de hombre, más afilados que esos poemas,
ingenuos y lamentables, que ustedes
se pasan el día escribiendo.

Los hemos respetado más de sesenta minutos,
un tiempo suficiente para la poesía,
palabras mejor escritas a raíz de una emoción,
un pensamiento. Demasiado pesimistas unos
y mucho más optimistas otros.
Hemos sufrido escuchándolos, sabiendo que detrás,
en una mesa larga, hay dispuestas copas y cubiertos.
Música, lámparas, serpentinas, globos, estrellas.
El fin de estos propósitos es por supuesto el brindis.

Deténganse, no sigan leyendo. Por el bien de nosotros,
y de ustedes. No sigan leyendo y tampoco escribiendo.
Recuerden que el futuro, emoción y pensamiento,
depende más de ustedes que de cualquier otro hombre.
Queridos escritores de todas partes del mundo,
observen nuestros dientes mientras aplaudimos.

The quantity of water initially necessary to support the substratum is determined by its nature and dimensions

Dear writers all over the world,
so beautifully made up and turned out,
ironed and starched,
timid and eccentric:

hurry it up.

Or just stop reading – stop at once.
Spare a thought for the audience
(the *highly dangerous* audience)
who have come to listen to you.
They have shark teeth, crocodile teeth, panther teeth,
dog teeth and human teeth, teeth
sharper than those poems
(those earnest, deplorable poems)
you spend all day writing.

We have indulged you for more than an hour now,
which is time enough for poetry.
All the best words for this emotion,
that thought. Some a tad pessimistic,
some extravagantly optimistic,
we have suffered them all.
We have suffered them all,
knowing all the while
that behind us is a long table
set with glasses and cutlery.
Music, lights, balloons, streamers, stars.
The finale, of course, is the drinks reception.

So stop right there – don't read another word.
For our sake, and for yours. Don't read another word
and don't write any either. But remember:

the future, and all emotion and all thought,
depend more on you than on any other human being.
Dear writers all over the world,

look at our teeth as we applaud.

Abuelo Brecht

Resulta que el teatro posdramático es un teatro de libertad,
un teatro humano.
Por lo que si me coloco en el centro de la escena
seré un ser humano libre.
Es el tipo de teatro que me conviene.
Y le conviene a mi familia. El problema es convencer
a mi familia de que se trasladen hasta aquí:
el centro de la escena.
Mi familia está formada por más de seis integrantes.
Habría que alquilar un camión, o un tráiler,
o por lo menos
un coche motor. Habría que vender la vivienda antigua
en la que ha nacido el resto de los integrantes,
incluso yo.
Y así lograr proveernos de alimentos. Brecht
y sus seguidores desarrollaron un tipo de teatro abominable
que se traduce como teatro didáctico. Un teatro
hecho para la misma gente que lo hace.
Encuentro contradicción en ello pero pongo punto en boca.
Brecht es el más viejo de mis familiares.

Grandpa Brecht

It turns out postdramatic theatre is a theatre of freedom,
a human theatre.
So if I put myself centre stage
I will be a free human being.
This is a kind of theatre I can get along with.
My family could get along with it too. The problem
is convincing my family to relocate here:
centre stage.
My family is made up of more than six people.
They'd have to hire a lorry, or a trailer,
at the very least
a motor car. They'd have to sell the old homestead
where all the other members of my family were born,
me included.
That's how we'd provide for ourselves. Brecht
and his followers developed a terrible kind of theatre
which is really a theatre of instruction; a theatre
made for the same people that make it.
There is a contradiction in this, but I'll keep schtum.
Of all my relatives, Brecht is the oldest.

Cubo, soga, extintor, etc.

En murales contra incendios aparecen accesorios
necesarios para el caso,
como el cubo, la soga, el extintor,
la manta, el teléfono, el pico, la pala, y la arena.

Cada centro de trabajo ambiciona
su mural con los objetos de ejemplo.
El que no contemple objetos
aparece rezagado en una emulación
a ratos mensual y a ratos semestral.

Los centros de trabajo que más puntuación
ganen en la emulación,
resultan centros de trabajo destacados.

El recurso humano involucrado
recibe del resto de los recursos una felicitación cordial.

Al producirse el incendio los accesorios de ejemplo
no deben extraerse del mural.

Bucket, rope, fire extinguisher, etc.

On fire safety signs you can see all the items
needed for the occasion:
bucket, rope, fire extinguisher,
blanket, telephone, shovel, pick, and sand.

Every workplace must have a sign
with all its example items.
If you're not familiar with said items,
you won't be up to speed
for the sometimes-monthly sometimes-weekly fire drill.

The workplaces that score highest in the fire drill
are considered the most distinguished workplaces.

The human resources involved
get a cheery congratulations from all the other human resources.

In the event of a fire, example items
may not be taken from the fire safety sign.

Me estoy haciendo amiga de todos los policías de la ciudad para después asaltar un banco con mi pistola de agua

Nadie se mata con una pistola de agua
a no ser que en vez de agua
rellene la pistola con cuarenta
mililitros de ácido muriático o espíritu de sal
y se la ponga en la boca.

I'm making friends with all the police in the city so I can rob a bank with my water pistol

No one gets killed with a water pistol
unless, instead of water,
they fill the pistol with forty
millilitres of hydrochloric acid
and put it in their mouth.

Importancia y desarrollo de la tolerancia

Criando pollos de granja no se llega a ningún lado.
Le dijo el mejor amigo de mi papá a mi papá.

Aquí en esta casa cada uno tiene un baño.
Le dijo la madre de mi papá a mi papá.

La casa de tus hijas es también tu casa.
Le dijo mi mamá a mi papá.

Ahora tu madre soy yo.
Le dijo mi mamá a mi papá.

Nosotros somos tus hijos.
Le dijeron muy solemnes los treinta pollos de granja.

El hombre se echó en lo oscuro.
Empezó a cerrar los ojos después del minuto y medio.

The importance of tolerance and its development

Keeping chickens won't get you anywhere,
said my dad's best friend to my dad.

In this house everyone has their own bathroom,
said my dad's mother to my dad.

Your daughters' home is also your home,
said my mum to my dad.

I am your mother now,
said my mum to my dad.

We are your children,
said the thirty chickens, very solemnly.

The man threw himself into the dark.
After a minute or two he began to close his eyes.

Tesoro del agricultor

La noche camagüeyana, noche universal,
está llena de vínculos entre una cosa y otra.
Fiebre de cocodrilo, fiebre engañosa,
en el termómetro que me pongo bajo la lengua.
Manuales para el cultivo de las principales plantas
propias de los climas tropicales, escritos
por el Dr. Francisco Javier Balmaseda,
Caballero Condecorado por el Gobierno
de la República Francesa con la
CRUZ DEL MÉRITO AGRÍCOLA.
Lágrimas de polvo de cemento
utilizado en la construcción de paredes improvisadas
para una mejor convivencia de tres generaciones juntas.
Un hombre dando azadón
sobre la tierra de un patio abonado con basura.
Semillas esparcidas desde las manos de un hombre
empecinado en sacarle cualquier jugo a la tierra.
Fiebre de cocodrilo, cocodrilo de tierra, tierra y agua.
Es de noche, hombre.
La noche es el tesoro del agricultor.

Farmer's treasure

Camagueyan night, universal night,
strung with links between one thing and another.
Crocodile fever, delirium fever,
says the thermometer under my tongue.
Manuals for the cultivation of crops
in tropical climates, written
by Dr Francisco Javier Balmaseda, Gentleman,
Decorated by the Government
of the French Republic, with the
CROSS OF AGRICULTURAL MERIT.
Cement teardrops
for the construction of makeshift walls
where three generations are living together.
A man, taking a mattock
to the earth of a garden
fertilised with rubbish.
Seeds, scattered
from the hands of the man
who is bent
on getting at some slender root.
Crocodile fever.
Earth crocodile, earth and water.
Night, man.
Night is the farmer's treasure.

CHUPAR LA PIEDRA
SUCKING THE STONE

La dulce vida

Durante el año 1507
alguien llamado Alberto Durero me pintó
la obra se llama Retrato de muchacha (o muchacho) y es un
    pergamino aplicado sobre tela
él también pintó a Los cuatro jinetes del Apocalipsis hace poco los
    cuatro jinetes y yo nos hicimos amigos después de cinco siglos
    exactos
me pasa que me enamoro de uno de los jinetes
pero el jinete ya tiene novia
pero yo estoy tan arrinconada
tan arrinconada tan arrinconada
y tomo el auricular y le digo a Alberto Durero:
voy a picarme el muslo
con la misma cuchilla que afilabas tus carbones
con la sangre de mi muslo
Alberto Durero pinta una obra
llamada El jinete y la muchacha
donde aparecemos el jinete y yo
conversando seriamente sobre la dulce vida
el jinete engulle frutas
y a mí se me salen los leucocitos
Alberto Durero piensa:
esta muchacha parece tonta
ni a mí se me ocurriría llorar
frente a uno de los jinetes del Apocalipsis definitivamente no se me
    ocurriría
y tomo el auricular y le digo a Alberto Durero: la dulce vida y yo no
    tenemos parecido

The good life

In the year 1507
I was painted by someone called Albrecht Dürer
the painting is *Portrait of a Young Girl* (or *Boy*)
                    – parchment mounted on canvas
Dürer also painted *The Four Horsemen of the Apocalypse*
and at some point the Four Horsemen and I got to be friends
    exactly five centuries later
it turns out I'm in love with one of the Horsemen
but the Horseman already has a girlfriend
and I'm the odd one out –
I'm left on the shelf, put in the corner,
so I pick up the phone and I say to Dürer
I'm going to prick my thigh
with that same knife you use to sharpen your charcoal
and with the blood of my thigh
Albrecht Dürer paints a painting called
The Horseman and the Young Girl
in which it looks as if the Horseman and I
are having a serious conversation about the good life
the Horseman is guzzling fruit
and I am leaking leucocytes
Albrecht Dürer thinks
this girl looks like a complete berk
but I wouldn't dream of crying
in front of one of the Horsemen of the Apocalypse no way not in a
    million years
so I pick up the phone and I say to Dürer
the good life and I bear no resemblance to one another

Los caminos

El cofre donde guardé
aquellos pedazos de vidrio
con forma de animales cabizbajos apareció en la calle
roto
y los vidrios
o los animales más hermosísimos del fin han empezado a meterse
hacia adentro
el cofre apareció en la calle penosamente roto
dejaré las cosas
como están
hasta que un día
aparezca yo en la calle
rota

The ways

The casket
in which I kept those little pieces of glass
in the shape of gloomy animals
has turned up in the street

broken

and the bits of glass
the most gorgeous animals
lady birds and slow worms
had just begun to make themselves at home in there

the casket turned up in the street *meticulously* broken

I will leave everything
exactly as it is
until the day
I turn up in the street

broken

No se cómo ponerle a este poema

Los ratones que me comieron la lengua
se llamaban Arsénico, Ventrílocuo y Ámbar
yo dejé que me comieran la lengua
para enfermarlos
porque mi lengua tenía el mal de la trasgresión mi bella lengua nació
    transgresora
y lo que nace, crece
hasta que ya no me cupo en el túnel
tuve que mudarme a un cubículo más amplio
y luego a un parque
y luego a un monte
mi bella lengua se subía en los jagüeyes también en la yagruma
se subía además en la majagua
desde allí maleducaba al mundo
todo con mis órganos a rastro
entonces me cansé

I don't know how to put this

The rats that ate my tongue
were called Arsenic, Ventriloquist and Amber
and I let them eat my tongue
to make them sick
because my tongue had the blight of transgression my beautiful
    tongue was born transgressive
and what is born, grows
so now it won't fit in its shaft
I had to move to a bigger cubicle
then to a park
then out to the country
my beautiful tongue climbed the *jagüeys* and it climbed the *yagruma*
and it climbed the *majagua* too
and from there it corrupted the world
all this with my organs hanging out
                    then I got tired

La ley de la dinámica

Con Galileo no puedo juntarme
ninguno de los dos sabemos trabajar
(Galileo no tiene casa
y yo sembré una grosella en el patio
pero tampoco sirvió)
te lo dije mil veces Galileo
que te pusieras la pulsa de santajuanas y mates
que orinaras en mi boca cuando la luna menguara
que me dijeras que somos los sinónimos del éxtasis pero tampoco
con Galileo no puedo ni bailar la macarena
te lo dije mil veces Galileo
la macarena es un baile para calientes o sátiros
la macarena es el límite del amor que nos teníamos
y el amor que nos tenemos desde el tufo por la noche un tufo a
    macabros huecos por donde se filtra el ámbar y también las
    ambivalencias del amarillo al ceder
te lo dije mil veces Galileo
es necesario ceder
con Galileo no puedo ceder
mañana me invitará a deslizarnos
en una penca de yagua
y todo sucederá distinto a su teoría
el monte se llenará de trivialidades
y yo me desnudaré
dejándome solamente los zapatos ortopédicos sin embargo las
    aguas oxidarán mis zapatos tú te irás Galileo
a vivir entre residuos

The law of dynamics

I can't get together with Galileo –
neither of us knows how to do anything useful
(Galileo doesn't have a house
and I planted a redcurrant bush on the patio
but that wasn't any good either)
I've told you a thousand times, Galileo
put on your bracelet of santajuanas and onyx
piss in my mouth when the moon is on the wane
tell me we're synonyms for ecstasy, but
no, I can't dance the Macarena with you, Galileo
I've told you a thousand times, Galileo
the Macarena is a dance for satyrs and other sex-mad creatures
the Macarena is all our love ever was
and the love we have
from volcanic ash at night volcanic cinders
to macabre holes through which filters amber
and also the ambivalences of yellow and surrender
I've told you a thousand times, Galileo
it is necessary to surrender
I can't surrender with Galileo
            tomorrow he will invite me
to slide with him on a palm tree leaf
and everything will happen to contradict his theory
the countryside will be filled with trivialities
and I will take my clothes off
leaving only my orthopaedic shoes although the water will rust my
    shoes and you
you will go, Galileo
and live among the ruins

Chupar la piedra

Al citrino lo chupo con cuatro lenguas la lengua de la palabra
la lengua de la salud
la lengua del frenesí
y la lengua del conocimiento
aparentemente una de las lenguas
está dividida en dos
tampoco la mandarria tritura al lapislázuli
por el contrario
lo quiebra dulcemente y le da poderes húmedos
le da el don de los sueños
el don de la tierra
el don de las ciudades con límites y flora
nadie ve al lapislázuli debajo de mí
nadie me ve
por eso no la he chupado
aunque sé que la venturina tiene sabor a oxígeno
a mí carente de oxígeno
me falta eso que las muchachas llaman habilidades no soy habilidosa
      pero soy amorosa
y el amor es señal de sabiduría

Sucking the stone

I suck the citrine with four tongues   the tongue of language
the tongue of health
the tongue of frenzy
and the tongue of knowledge
apparently one of these tongues
is forked
the mallet does not pulverise lapis lazuli
on the contrary
it breaks it sweetly and gives it wet potencies
it gives it the gift of dreaming
the gift of earth
the gift of cities with outskirts and flora
no one sees the lapis lazuli underneath me
no one sees me at all
for this reason I have not sucked it
though I know that venturine tastes like oxygen
like my lack of oxygen
I lack what the girls call *skills*
I'm not skilled but I'm loving
and love is a sign of wisdom

Teatro Kabuki

La cama continúa siendo cama
y el libro continúa siendo libro
y yo sentada en un parque lleno de llaves de oro
no debería beber hasta el alba pero en fin
hay entre los pájaros un artículo de peluquería
un adorno en mi cabeza
cuántas veces he querido arreglarme la cabeza
no existe la cabeza
mi topacio es un pez telescópico el lunes
un tiburón el martes
un salmón el miércoles
un bello marisco el jueves
mi topacio el viernes es una anguila
y el sábado un manjuarí
estoy híbrida en un parque lleno de piedras artificiales pensé: la
    noche es un símbolo
que ninguna civilización supera
nadie supera y por eso estoy muy híbrida
muy poco disponible
pensé: la cama es un símbolo
yo misma soy una cama demasiado alucinante
aunque todos absolutamente todos
nos levantemos de ella

Kabuki theatre

The bed carries on being a bed
and the book carries on being a book
and there's me sat in a park filled with golden keys
I don't *have* to drink till dawn, but hey
in among the birds is a hair accessory
a decoration for my head
how many times have I wanted to get my head straight
my head does not exist
my topaz
is a goldfish on Mondays
a shark on Tuesdays
a salmon on Wednesdays
a beautiful shellfish on Thursdays
on Fridays my topaz is an eel
and on Saturdays a garfish
and here's me drunk in a park filled with artificial stones   I thought:
    night is a symbol
no civilisation can embellish
that no one can embellish, and that's why I'm half cut
out to lunch
I thought: the bed is a symbol
I myself am a pretty spectacular bed
although everyone, absolutely everyone,
    gets out of it

Chupar la piedra

Estando abierta
todos ven que me cabe un escritorio
un ventilador de pie
y otros objetos desconocidos
estando abierta creo en la palabra
y lleno la habitación de piedras
para esculpir la palabra
estando abierta tú también me cabes
cerrada no
cerrada no podré representar
hoy me sacaré los dientes
con unos alicates de jardín
compro alicates de jardín
compro un escritorio y un ventilador de pie estando cerrada
mi lengua se vuelve un gancho
cuya primera función es chupar la piedra
en la piedra escribí palabras
las palabras han formado
el concepto de erotismo
mis palabras han formado un erotismo verbal estando cerrada mato
    diez pájaros
abierta no

Sucking the stone

Being open
everyone can see I can manage a writing desk
a pedestal fan
and other unknown objects

being open I believe in words
and fill the room with stones
in order to sculpt words

being open I can also manage you
not when I'm closed
when closed, I can't perform

today I will take out my teeth
with a pair of secateurs
I buy a pair of secateurs
I buy a writing desk and a pedestal fan   being closed
my tongue becomes a hook
whose primary function is sucking the stone
on the stone I wrote words
the words have regrouped
as the concept of eroticism
my words have formed a verbal eroticism   being closed I kill ten
    birds stone dead
not when I'm open

El mundo de los sentidos

La presencia de geométricos objetos sobre el ventanal del porche
nunca ha interrumpido
mis horarios de lectura
sino que he disfrutado de las letras como mismo se disfruta un baile
ayer aparecieron objetos diferentes geométricos y estáticos pero
    diferentes yo voy a bailar contigo
sobre la piedra amatista de mi simbología bailaremos huapango,
    jarabe, bamba, chapaneca y raspa, sandunga y jarana sumaremos
    nuestros cuerpos
a la geométrica obra y nos pareceremos muy poco

The world of the senses

The presence of geometric shapes over the large window of the
    porch
has never interrupted
my reading
    on the contrary I have always enjoyed letters as one enjoys a dance
yesterday different geometric shapes appeared, static
                        but different I am going to dance with you
on the amethyst of my system of symbols   we will dance huapango,
jarabe, bamba,
        chapaneca and raspa,
                    sandunga and jarana   we will join our bodies
        to the geometric work and we will look nothing like each other

Cuatro por cuatro

Los cuatro dientes cariados de mi boca serán enterrados en un pozo
    sin fondo
no hay vasija en el pozo para sacar el agua pero tampoco hay agua
    en el pozo
las cuatro maquinarias de mi eje
serán enterradas en un jardín
del jardín no hablaré porque ya un pintor lo hizo y hasta llenó el
    jardín de gente
mis maquinarias ahuyentarán la tiniebla
para ser mejores maquinarias
las cuatro personalidades de mi espíritu serán enterradas
bajo las cuatro personalidades de tu espíritu los cuatro pares saldrán
    a caminar
por una carretera larga
el resto será enterrado entre las piedras comunes las piedras
    comunes me taparán los ojos

Four by four

The four rotten teeth in my head will be buried in a bottomless well
there is no bucket in the well to draw water
                                but then there's no water in the well either
the four mechanisms of my axle
will be buried in a garden
I will not speak of the garden because a painter has already done so
                                and even filled the garden with people
my mechanisms will keep the darkness away
in order to be better mechanisms
the four personalities of my spirit will be buried
beneath the four personalities of your spirit
                                        the four pairs will go out walking
down a long road
everything else
will be buried among the common stones the common stones
                                        will be placed over my eyes

**HILO+HILO
THREAD+THREAD**

El hilo

Yo jamás había visto un hilo en una vagina
colgando de la vagina como un moco de catarro
como un pañuelo de fiebre
yo jamás había halado un hilo de una vagina
se le iba a salir el alma
se le iba a ir con el hilo la memoria del horror
yo lo halé aquella noche
lo halé con la boca
y fue la primera vez que me arrepentí de algo.

The thread

I'd never seen a thread in a vagina
hanging from the vagina like a gob of mucus
like a white handkerchief
I'd never pulled a thread from a vagina
      the soul would come out with it
the memory of horror would come out with the thread
I pulled on it that night
I pulled it with my mouth
and it was the first time I ever regretted anything.

Para tener lo que me fue dado

Una mujer que llora es un hombre desnudo y feo
una mujer que fuma es un niño caprichoso
una mujer que mea es una mala estructura
una mujer que muere es otra mujer
una mujer de afuera puede bailar al ritmo
de los blancos y los negros
de afuera significa extraña
de afuera quiere decir de un lugar extraño y dulce
una mujer extraña es un hombre vestido y bello
una mujer que piensa es una rana en el fango
una mujer que singa
piensa.

To get what I'm given

A woman who cries is an ugly, naked man
a woman who smokes is a petulant child
a woman who pisses is a bad structure
a woman who dies is another woman
an outsider woman can dance to the rhythm
of black or white
outsider means exotic
outside means somewhere sweet and strange
a foreign woman is a beautiful and well-dressed man
a woman who thinks is a frog in the mud
a woman who fucks
thinks.

El frío bajo la luna

Los huesos que traquean hacen ruidos que dan asco
la vida es una tendencia a sentir asco por muchos ruidos
sucede porque a la muerte las mujeres y los hombres van
desnudos
y dejan de ser tendenciosos para ser amables
y lo que alguna vez hizo ruido ya se ha quedado en silencio
finalmente el asco desembocando en arqueada
ahuyenta la armonía de los hombres
sustrae excitación en las mujeres
genitales de mujeres y genitales de hombres
sufren el frío bajo la luna del fin
los huesos se separan y no hay nada que esperar.

Cold beneath the moon

Cracking joints make a disgusting noise
life is essentially a tendency to be disgusted by many noises
this is because men and women
go naked unto death, at which point
they stop being tendentious and start being kind
and everything that once made a noise falls silent

in the end, disgust gives way to retching
it shatters men's harmony
it numbs women's arousal
the genitals of women and the genitals of men
suffer the inevitable cold beneath the moon
and the bones come apart and there's nothing to hope for.

El colmo

La buena memoria de una mujer
hace que no olvide a su primer amor
y ese todavía no es el colmo
hace que recuerde la primera película
el primer libro
los primeros golpes
en la cara
y ese todavía no es el colmo
hace que vuelva la vista atrás
y vea pasar sus años
desde el huevo de su madre
hasta hoy
y ese todavía no es el colmo
hace que el resto de las mujeres
giren en torno a su memoria
y eso no es nada
en comparación
con su memoria
hace que el primer amor
sea una mancha indestructible
y que el último
más.

The worst part

A woman never forgets
so she'll never forget her first love
and that's not the worst part

she'll always remember that first film
that first book
those first blows
to the face
and that's not the worst part

she must look back
and watch all her years pass before her
from her mother's gonads
right up till now
and that's not the worst part

all the other women
hang around in her memory
and that's nothing
compared to her memory

making her first love
an indelible stain

and her last love
all the more so.

Labios

Que a una mujer
le chupen las tetas
pezones, aureola y borde
significa que pierda el camino
y lo recupere
mientras le siguen chupando
pezones, aureola
pero que una mujer
le chupe las tetas a otra
significa que pierda todo
y lo recupere
y pierda todo
y lo recupere
y cuando lo recupere
se dé cuenta de que todo
no era nada
comparado con el resto.

Lips

when a woman
has her tits sucked
    nipples, aureoles, all
    around the perimeter
she loses her way
then finds it again
all the while
having her tits sucked
    nipples, aureoles
but when a woman
sucks another woman's tits
she loses everything
and finds it again
and loses everything
and finds it again
and when she finds it again
she realises *everything*
    is nothing
compared to everything *else*.

Fácil

A una mujer tú la tocas
y ella tiembla
la escupes y ella sale
empapada en saliva
a una mujer tú la puedes
destruir
¿cómo la destruyes?
fácil
la tocas
y la escupes
la tocas
y la escupes
la tocas
y la escupes
entre una cosa y otra
le dices que de pronto
has empezado a quererla
que simplemente
la quieres
y ya
por último la tocas
y la escupes.

Easy

Touch a woman
and she trembles

spit her out
and she comes out
covered in spit

you can of course
destroy a woman
how to destroy her?
easy –

you touch her
you spit her out
you touch her
you spit her out
you touch her
between one
and the other
you tell her
that all of a sudden
you have fallen in love with her
that quite simply
you love her
and then
one last time

touch her
and spit her out.

Cómo suenan los violins

La pasión por el ser amado
hace que uno ponga la boca
en lugares que no se hicieron
para poner la boca
una verruga en el cuello
no se hizo para poner la boca
un golondrino en la axila
no se hizo para poner la boca
ni una ñáñara de caspa
ni un lunar de sangre
abultado
iniciar la noche
apasionadamente
y ver el hongo
en el pie del ser amado
hace que uno ponga la boca
en el hongo.

How the violin sounds

Passion for your beloved
makes you put your mouth
in places where mouths
are not supposed to be put

you are not supposed to put your mouth
on a wart on a neck
you are not supposed to put your mouth
on a bubo in an armpit
not on a flaking scalp
not on a blood blister
          swollen
in the preamble
to a night of passion
and spotting a fungal infection
on the foot of your beloved

you put your mouth
right there in the fungus.

Los kilómetros

Lo lógico en un hombre que va por una línea
es que pierda el equilibrio y caiga
comprendiendo que la tierra es una superficie
buena para sus pies y buena para sus manos
para un hombre que va por la tierra
a veces con los pies y a veces con las manos
no es lógico que pierda el equilibrio y caiga
comprendiendo que la tierra es una superficie
engañosa y común
y que una línea hubiera sido recta
para mí que perdí las piernas
y luego perdí los brazos
y luego el corazón
la lógica no indica nada.

Kilometres

It's logical that a man who walks a line
should lose his balance and fall
knowing all the while
that the earth is a surface
that is good for the feet
and good for the hands
of a man who walks the earth
sometimes on his feet
and sometimes on his hands

it's not logical
to lose one's balance and fall
knowing that the earth
is a shared and treacherous surface

or that the line should be straight
for me, who lost her legs
and then her arms
and then her heart

logic doesn't prove anything.

La casa

Mi casa es un hombre
mi casa es una mujer
tanto uno como el otro son mi casa
el tiempo y el espacio
da lo mismo si duermo sobre un bíceps
o sobre un seno redondo
mi casa es mi vida
y mi muerte
en la casa de mis padres
había un lugar
donde llegado el momento
todo el mundo se moría
esa casa no era un hombre
ni era una mujer
esa casa era un niño
con miedo a la casa
en mi hombre y en mi mujer
ni siquiera hay muebles
aún.

The house

My house is a man
my house is a woman
both are my house
and time and space
are exactly the same
if I sleep on a bicep
or a lovely round breast
my house is my life
and my death

in my parents' house
was a place
where everyone went to die
that house
was not a man
or a woman
that house was a child
a child afraid of the house

my man and my woman
aren't even furnished
not yet.

Yo no existo

Aquí está la oreja
aquí está el cuello
aquí la nuca y el hombro
esto tan bonito es el pezón
esto de aquí
anegado en agua
es el ombligo
aquí está la ingle
pero en la ingle ni loca
aquí está la vulva
pero en la vulva ni loca
todavía
ni loca
aquí la pierna
y el tobillo
y la planta
estos son los labios
y esto es lo que da el afeite
aquí está el clítoris
y esto es lo que da el amor
una lengua entre los labios
sin comunicarse
las bajas pasiones
también existen.

I do not exist

Here is the ear
here is the neck
here is the nape of the neck
and the shoulder
this lovely thing here
is the nipple
and this here
flooded with water
this is the navel
here is the groin
(nope – not in the groin)
here is the vulva
(nope – not in the vulva
no
still no)
here is the leg
the ankle
the sole of the foot
these are the lips
and this is what shaving does
this is the clitoris
and this is what loving does
a tongue between lips
speechless

the base passions:
they too exist.

El hilo

Una vez vi un hilo colgando de una vagina
y lo halé pensando que de adentro
las cosas no se desprenden por gusto
no me arrepentí por lo que hubiera podido desprenderse
sino porque se desprendió algo insignificante
algo que hubiera podido ser el alma
pero que no fue el alma de ninguna manera
apenas un moco mal anudado.

The thread

Once I saw a thread hanging out of a vagina
and I pulled it, thinking
that things don't just *fall out* of a person
I didn't feel bad about what might have fallen out
but because something insignificant fell out
something that might have been a soul
but which was not a soul in any sense
                    just a badly knotted gob of mucus.

NOTES

FERTILE TRUCE: A note on the title

The so-called Rewarding Truce (*Tregua Fecunda*) refers to the seventeen years of Cuba's history between the cessation of the Ten Years War (1878) and the beginning of the War of Independence (1895).

Fertile Truce

The national flower of Cuba is the *mariposa*, or white ginger lily.

The use of the English *grandfather* in place of the Spanish *abuelo* plays on the idea of foreign intrusion and interference: a vexed issue for the revolutionary generation.

Memory is a bullet train

The Spanish word *afuera* means *outdoors, outside, out there*; it has a particular resonance in Cuban Spanish, connoting above all *out of Cuba*.

Spoilt

Hatibonico and Tínima are rivers flowing through Camagüey; Tínima is also the name of a pale lager brewed in the city.

Special Period

The Special Period refers to Cuba's years of economic crisis following the collapse of the Soviet Union.

The *tocororo*, or trogon, is the national bird of Cuba; its plumage resembles the colours of the Cuban flag.

Tilapia are a staple of Cuban aquaculture, imported and intensively bred to answer to the food shortages of the Special Period. Cultured tilapia in Cuba today are gene edited and hormonally modified to produce a predominantly male population; in this sense they *transform*.

Rotten cherry

The Avenida de los Presidentes is a broad avenue in the Vedado district of Havana, lined with statues of Cuba's Presidents and other Latin American leaders.

Canaan

Cuba has named its years ever since the Revolution: those mentioned in the poem are genuine.

The Royal Palm (*palma real*) is the national tree of Cuba. A pun is lost here, as the Spanish *real* means both *royal* and *real*.

47

The names listed here (and later in 54) are municipalities of Camagüey Province, of which there are a total of thirteen. Between the two poems, Legna names twelve of them; the thirteenth municipality shares a name with the Province itself.

54

Camiones are Soviet-era trucks, manufactured in Russia or China, now repurposed as buses.

Más allá is the Spanish equivalent of the Latin *plus ultra*, the national motto of Spain. *Plus ultra* inverts the phrase *Non terrae plus ultra* (No land further beyond), said to have been inscribed on the Pillars of Hercules at the limit of the known world. It was adopted as a personal motto by Charles I of Spain following Columbus' journey to the New World; it connotes global endeavour and Spanish Imperialism.

Miami Century Fox: A note on the form

Miami Century Fox is a collection of fifty-one Petrarchan sonnets. Achy Obejas, who selected the manuscript to win the Paz Prize for Poetry, observes in her introduction:

"How perfect, I thought, that Petrarch – who bridged the classical and the modern periods – should lend his poetic design to Legna, newly arrived, and still somewhere between here and there, now and then, now and tomorrow, Cuba and the US."

We therefore felt it was important to preserve the form in translation. The thing is, it's much easier to rhyme in Spanish than in English; as a result, full English rhymes tend to sound more artificial. I've loosened the straps a little: I let myself off repeating the A and B rhymes in the second quatrain of the octave, and I've relied on slant and fuzzy rhymes to avoid unwelcome jingling.

Maggot People

Gusano (worm, maggot) is a slur used of Cubans who have defected from Cuba, and particularly those who left when Batista was overthrown.

Tarde mágica (Magic Afternoon) is a programming block of the Disney Junior channel in Latin America. The reference is lost outside of this geographical area, so I've swapped it out for Disney World's Magic Kingdom.

Ms Trolley remembers countries

Desaliento (dejection) contains a pun that's difficult to carry into English: the speaker is 'de-aliened', hence *settled*.

What is my name?

A *rollo* is a roll, as of barbed wire; figuratively, it also means a story or yarn.

Spelling Legna's name backwards provides a possible solution to the reference in line twelve: the archangel Michael is depicted wielding a sword as a symbol of righteous fury.

Giddy-up Johnny

Queso proceso was a kind of processed cheese eaten during the Special Period.

No flowers for me

Mammee is the mamey sapote, a tree native to Cuba, and also its sweet, creamy fruit, which is the national fruit of Cuba. Phonetically, it is almost identical to *mami* (mummy).

The head I lost

Vidrios calovares are sheets of reflective glass; these can be found fronting offices, hotels and government buildings in Cuba's cities.

GUM (NOW IS WHEN): A note on the title

The Spanish word *chicle* (chewing gum) is an anagram of *cliché*, a central concern of the collection.

My girlfriend leaves for Cancún today

At the time this poem was first published, the US position on Cuban immigration was known as the 'wet foot, dry foot policy'. Cubans intercepted at sea ('wet feet') were refused entry, while migrants who reached the shore ('dry feet') were permitted to remain and pursue residency. The term 'dusty foot' was used to describe Cubans entering the US via the border with Mexico. The wet foot, dry foot policy was revised by the Obama administration in 2017.

The ways

There are no *lady birds* or *slow worms* in Legna's original; these invasive species take the place of a pun that would otherwise be lost. 'Los caminos' contains a broken animal in the form of *del fin*: a *delfín* is a dolphin.

I don't know how to put this

Jagüey, *yagruma* and *majagua* are jungle trees found in Cuba.

The law of dynamics

Santajuanas are the seeds of the Santa Juana plant, commonly used in jewellery-making.

To get what I'm given

Here, *afuera* has multiple meanings. It retains its connotations of *outside Cuba*, but also suggests a woman outside of social conventions.

Abigail Parry

About the Authors

Legna Rodríguez Iglesias was born in Camagüey, Cuba in 1984. She works in a variety of genres, including poetry, short stories, novels, children's books and theatre. She has won a number of prestigious national and international prizes; most recently she was awarded the Premio Paz in 2016 in Miami for her collection of poems, *Miami Century Fox*.

Abigail Parry's first collection, *Jinx*, is published by Bloodaxe, and deals in trickery, gameplay, masks and costume. The poems have won a number of awards, including the Ballymaloe Prize, the Troubadour Prize and an Eric Gregory Award.

Serafina Vick graduated from King's College London in 2015 with a First Class degree in French and Hispanic Studies. She started translating Cuban poetry in 2014 whilst studying in Havana. Her translations have been featured in Modern Poetry in Translation and Bogota 39, and on BBC Radio 4. She lives in Havana, where she's currently working on her first novel.